I0825319

THE WORLD BEFORE RACISM

AN ART STORY

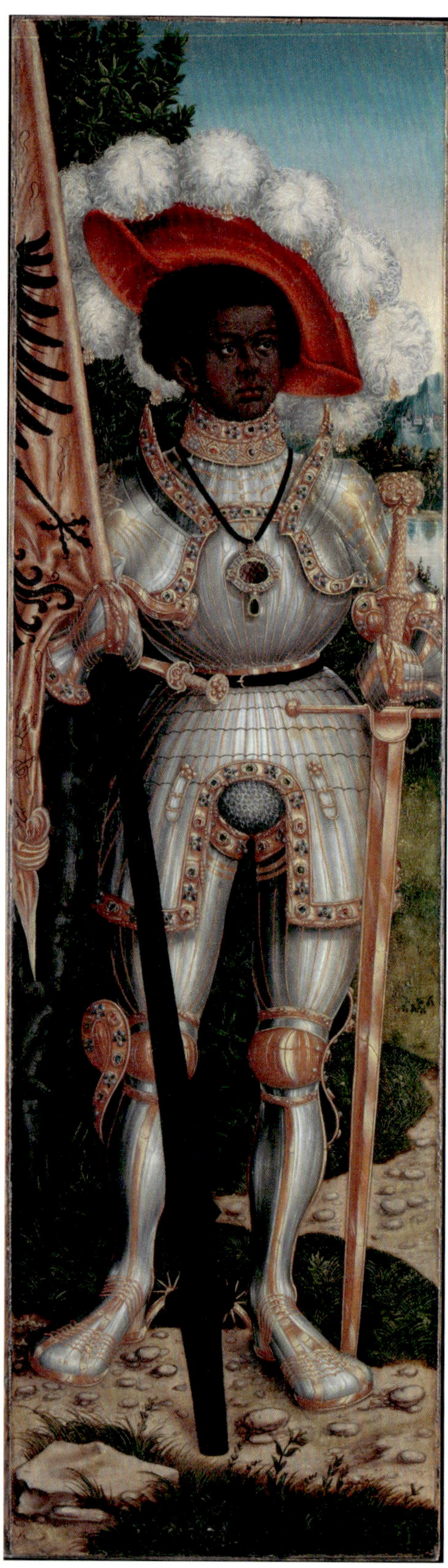

THE WORLD BEFORE RACISM

AN ART STORY

by LISA E. FARRINGTON, PhD

foreword by ERIN THOMPSON, PhD

introduction by JACK FLAM, PhD

The Artist Book Foundation
Manchester, Vermont

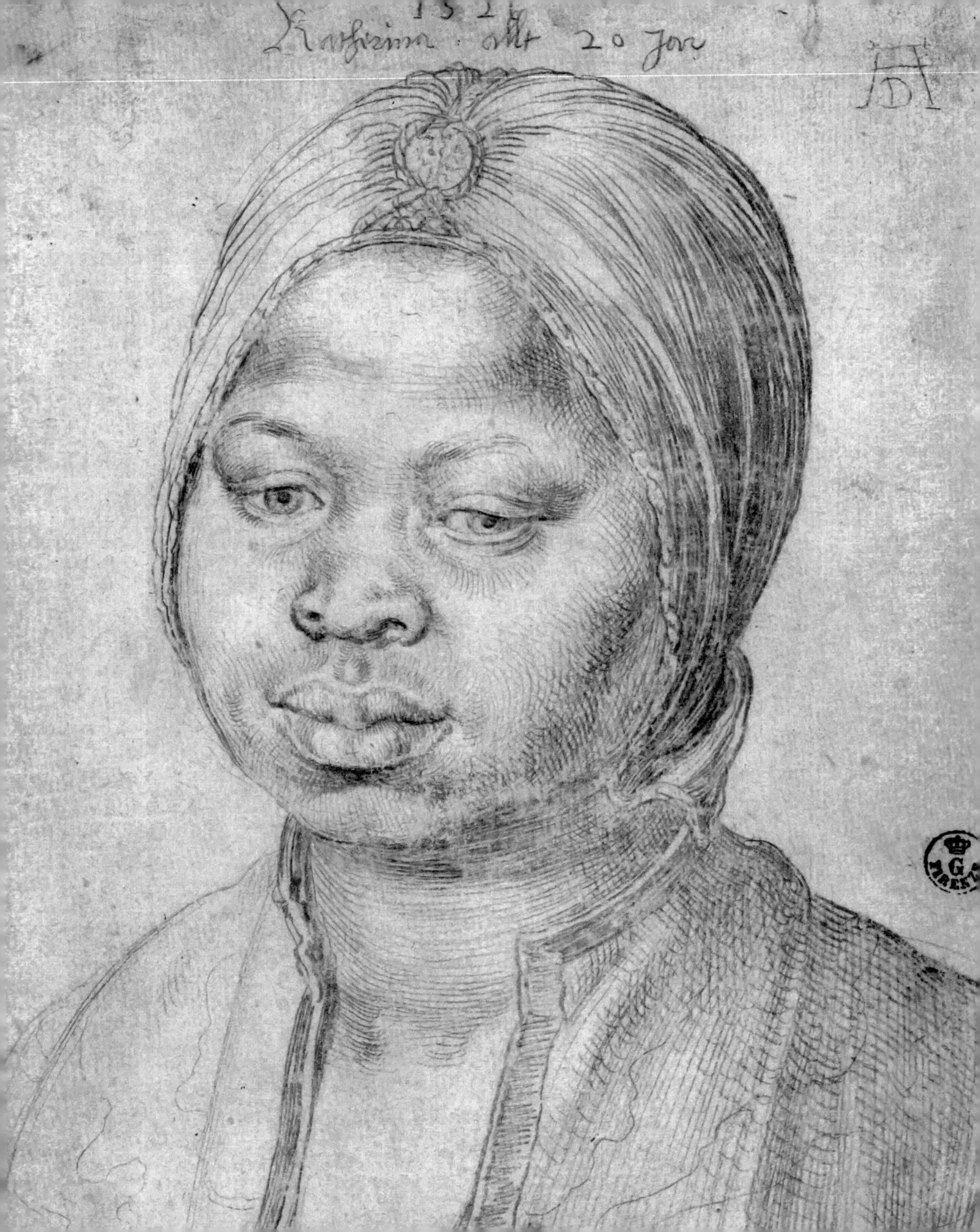

THE WORLD BEFORE RACISM

AN ART STORY

This book is dedicated to my late, beloved William "Billy Mazz" Mazzella who, for so many years, elevated my life and my soul.

– Lisa E. Farrington

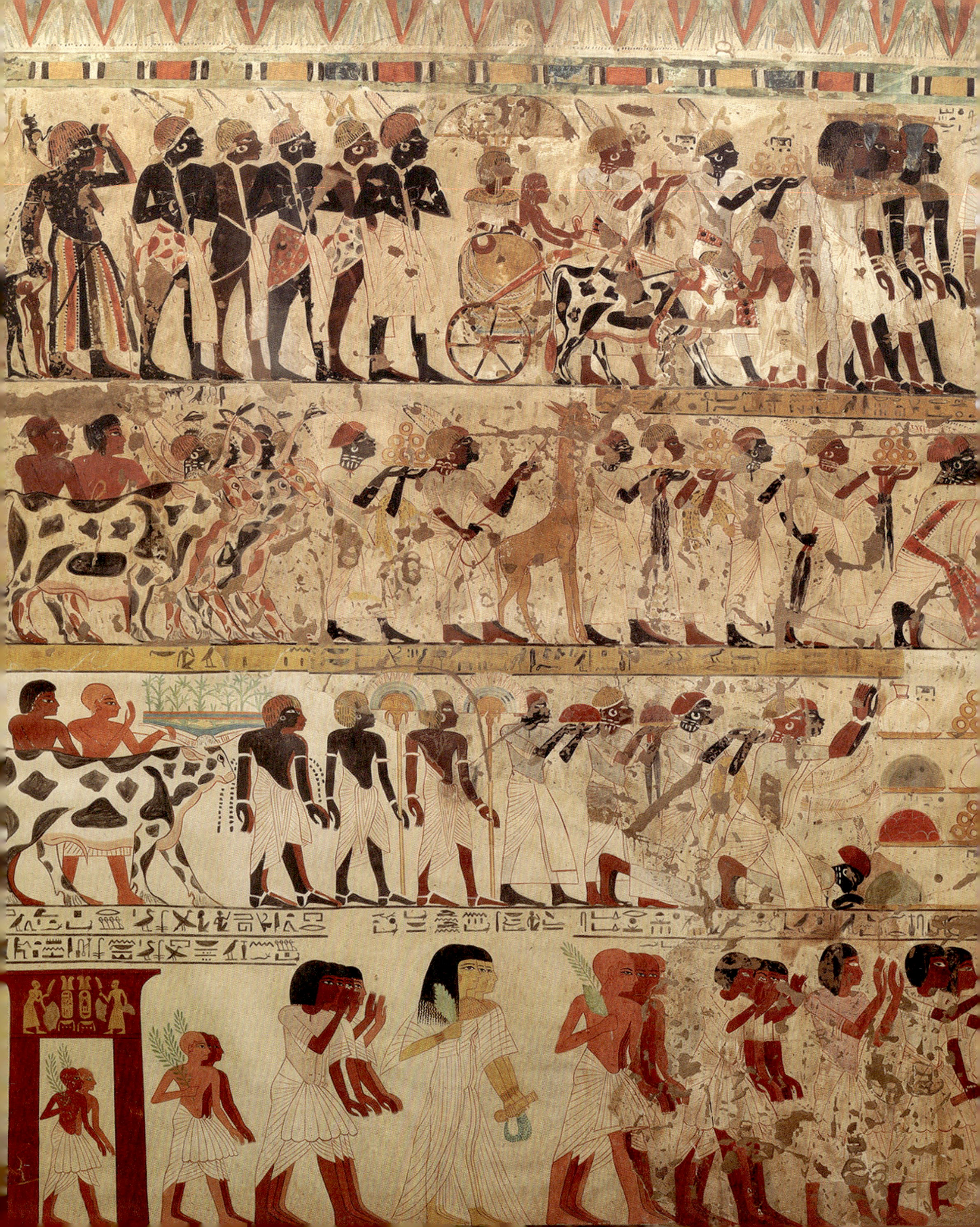

Foreword

ERIN THOMPSON, PhD

Charles K. Wilkinson, *Nubian Tribute Presented to the King*, ca. 1923–1927 (detail)
Tempera on paper
71 5/8 in. x 206 5/16 in. (182 x 524 cm)
Wall paintings from Tomb of Huy, Viceroy of Nubia buried at Qurnat Murai, New Kingdom, Dynasty 18, reigns of Thutmose IV and Amenhotep III, 1353–1327 BCE, Thebes, Upper Egypt
Metropolitan Museum of Art, New York, NY
Rogers Fund, 1930; acc. no. 30.4.21

In *The World Before Racism: An Art Story*, Lisa Farrington examines the fascinating and complex topic of the representation of Black subjects in art. Her work reminds me of how the award-winning author and sculptor Barbara Chase-Riboud summarizes her artistic projects as one of walking forgotten people "through the front door of history."[1] While Chase-Riboud, through the use of fiction and visual creativity to fill in erased histories, pries open what had been a barred entrance, Farrington's deep research recovers the facts of lives nearly lost to scholarly and cultural oblivion, from the Nubians who appeared in the carvings of ancient Egypt, to the Africans who were a vital part of the cultural life of ancient Greece and Rome, to the colonized subjects who asserted their dignified humanity in Victorian-era newspaper illustrations.

In recent years, protests around the world have led to the removal or modification of hundreds of statues honoring enslavers and colonizers, as well as to the launch of projects to fill these empty pedestals with sculptures that better reflect our multiracial world. Similarly, pressure to diversify the artwork on display in museums has resulted in rehangs of the permanent installations of several of these prominent institutions, with more to come. Increasing numbers of us are seeing ourselves in art and we can envision a place for ourselves in academia or curatorship.

These changes are admirable. But they should not be merely cosmetic. To change, we must fully recognize the deep linkages of the history of artistic representation of Black subjects to theories of racial inferiority used to justify exclusion and oppression. Farrington's book invites us to both see and overcome these connections. For example, she traces the history of images made to contrast African and European bodies and cultures from antiquity to the modern period, showing how ubiquitous such representations of "the other" have been in scientific, political, and decorative spheres. Our understanding of the world and each other is based on such cultural touchstones. If we hope to move toward true equality, we need to diagnose and reshape such underlying stereotypes.

If you study, create, or simply appreciate art and have been thinking about what needs to change in the ways we display, talk, and write about it, *The World Before Racism* will provide you with critical and relevant historical information. And if you study, create, or appreciate art and have not yet realized how urgent and crucial it is to make such changes, this book is certainly one you must read.

I was in the latter category when I first met Lisa Farrington. She was the chair of the art department at the college where I was interviewing for a professorship. When I came to campus, Farrington gave me a tour of an exhibition she had curated of the work of a major African American artist. She asked if I was familiar with this artist's work. Embarrassed, I had to admit that I was not. (So embarrassed, in fact, that I'm not going to tell you who the artist was.) "That's all right," she reassured me. Then she began to teach me. Learning from her is a privilege I have enjoyed thanks to our many years of working together—and now thanks to this book.

When I began working with Farrington I didn't know how lucky I was. She is one of only a handful of full professors of African descent working in the field of art history in America.[2] This reflects the lack of diversity in the art world as a whole. As of the last comprehensive survey,[3] less than 30 percent of American museum intellectual leaders (curatorial, education, conservation, and leadership staff) identify as people of color. More than 80 percent of the works in the collections of major American museums were made by White artists,[4] while a 2010 study estimated that nearly 80 percent of visitors to American museums were White.[5]

In the words of critic La Tanya S. Autry, museums are not neutral.[6] Nor is art history. In my years as an undergraduate and then a graduate student of art history, it is no exaggeration to say that I was taught about more artists whose first names were "Jacopo" than those with non-White identities.

I certainly did not learn of the great achievements Farrington covers in this book, ranging from the cities of sub-Saharan Africa to the paintings of modern masters.

But while art history, as an academic field, is a place of whiteness, the actual history of art is not. As Farrington makes clear in this book, African, and then African American, creators have always made major contributions to humanity's cultural heritage. Their work is even present, although hidden, in masterpieces of the European Renaissance that were often produced in part by enslaved artisans.

The World Before Racism is a guide to the many conversations all of us who love art must have about its future. This book will help light the way.

New York, NY
2024

NOTES

1. Barbara Chase-Riboud, *I Always Knew: A Memoir* (Princeton: Princeton University Press, 2022), 266. See also Suzette A. Spencer, "On Her Own Terms: An Interview with Barbara Chase-Riboud," *Callaloo* 32, no. 3 (Summer 2009): 736–757.

2. Seph Rodney, "Why Are There So Few Black Full Professors of Art History in the US?" *Hyperallergic*, November 30, 2015.

3. Liam Sweeney, Deirdre Harkins, and Joanna Dressel, "Report: Art Museum Staff Demographic Survey 2022" (New York and Washington DC: Ithaka S+R and American Alliance of Museums, 2022).

4. Chad M. Topaz et al., "Diversity of Artists in Major U.S. Museums," *PLOS One* 14, no. 3 (2019).

5. Betty Farrell and Maria Medvedeva, "Demographic Transformation and the Future of Museums" (Washington, DC: American Association of Museums, 2010).

6. La Tanya S. Autry and Mike Murawski, "Museums Are Not Neutral: We Are Stronger Together," *Panorama: Journal of the Association of Historians of American Art* 5, no. 2 (2019).

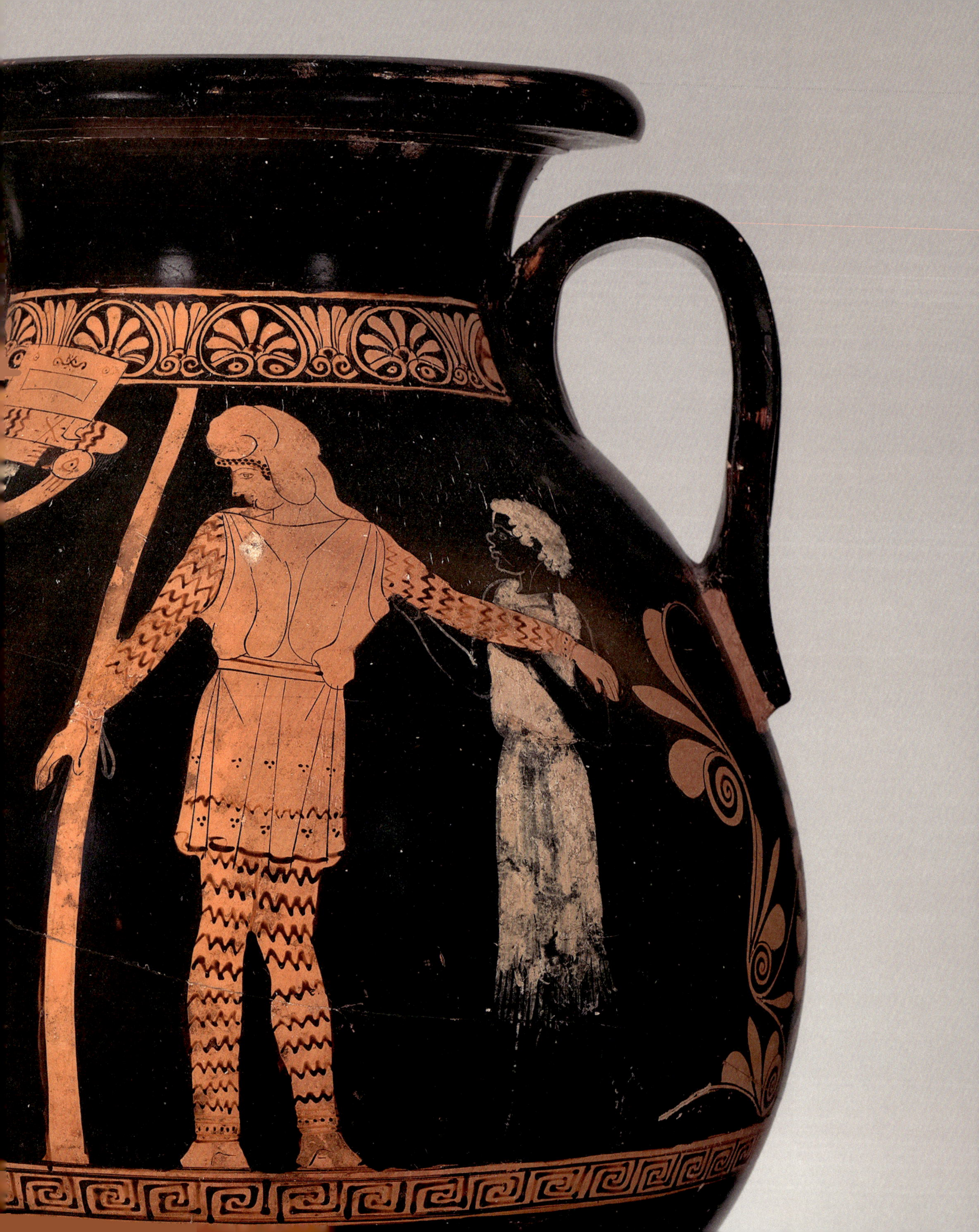

Introduction

JACK FLAM, PhD

The World Before Racism: An Art Story allows us to see racism, especially in the United States, in a bracingly fresh way. It locates an important transition in attitudes about race to the eighteenth century, and in doing so gives primacy to visual images, which are often free of the kind of spin that frequently exists in the overtly expressed attitudes of literary sources. As Lisa Farrington points out, we are able to look at works of visual art directly, without having to translate them from a foreign language, as well as with perhaps a greater awareness of their unconsciously implied perspectives than with the directly expressed, often polemical attitudes toward race and racism that we find in written texts.

In addressing these issues in a granular and personal way, this book also encourages us to reflect on our own attitudes and experiences of race and racism, and to rethink some of the assumptions and mistaken "facts" with which we have grown up. By doing so, it also provokes us to examine widespread attitudes toward culture and history in general.

Reading this book, for example, made me question why I — a reasonably well-educated former college professor who specialized in the history of modern art, with a sub-specialty in African culture — had not heard

Detail of *Pelike*, fig. 9, p. 27

until quite recently about such significant events in American history as the resentment-motivated massacres of financially successful Black people in Wilmington, North Carolina, in 1898 or in Tulsa, Oklahoma, in 1921; or, since I taught at the University of Florida for four years (1966–1970), why I'd never learned of the massacre that took place in the Black community of Rosewood, Florida, in 1923. Nor, to be honest, was I aware until recently of how extensive the anti-Black race riots of 1863 and 1919 had been in my own longtime home of New York City.

Reading this book also made me think of a number of incidents in my own life that now took on new resonance. Chief among these was the time in the spring of 1969 when I was invited to conduct a day-long seminar on African art, sponsored by the National Endowment for the Humanities, for members of the faculty at the historically Black Bethune-Cookman College (now Bethune-Cookman University) in Daytona Beach, Florida. At the end of the day, I was especially pleased when one of the African American faculty members invited me to have a drink with him. As we left the building, he said that I should follow him in my car, which surprised me, since we were near the center of one of the most well-known resort cities in the whole country.

I assumed that he wanted to go to a favorite local place, so I was even more surprised when we drove completely out of town, all the way to a Holiday Inn on I-95, the interstate highway. The dimly lit bar there had a kind of corporate elegance, which I figured was the reason we'd come all that way. But after we'd had a drink and made some small talk, he looked at me in a probing way and asked if I wondered why we'd come so far. It was, he told me, because he as a Black man would almost certainly have been refused service in downtown Daytona. But, he explained, since all the facilities on I-95 were effectively on federal land, the members of the staff there were strictly bound to serve Black people because of the 1964 federal Civil Rights Act.

Thinking about the Civil Rights Act brings to mind another experience I had in Florida around the same time as the one at Bethune-Cookman, when I was asked to testify as a character witness in a civil trial in the central Florida town of Tavares, which is the county seat of Lake County. While in the witness waiting area, I asked where I could get a drink of water and was directed to a pair of water fountains at the far end of the room. There, I was shocked to see that one was marked "White" and the other "Colored." Since the enforcement of this kind of segregation had not been legal for several years, it was clear that the signs on the fountains were intentionally left unchanged, as explicit reminders of how Blacks were to be regarded as separate and unequal, even in the county courthouse and despite what the law might actually be. The purpose behind such a reminder is similar to the way in which, after public hangings in England were abolished, the gibbets remained in place to remind people of how criminals had once been hanged and their corpses displayed in public.

Lisa Farrington's book makes us aware of how varying degrees of Otherness operate on both the social and economic levels. A sense of Us and Them may be deeply engrained in the human psyche, but as Farrington points out, the kind of extreme racism that has been prevalent in this country for the past three hundred years is another matter altogether. It is closely tied to economic interests and those deep economic interests—based initially on the free labor provided by slavery, and later on having a clearly identifiable class of people who can be "kept down"—have had a profound effect on almost every other aspect of American life, including politics, our system of justice, and religion. The political implications of racism, especially the denial of the right to vote, have become especially clear in recent years. And our system of justice is known not only to be stained by longstanding and widespread prejudice against Black people, but also to incarcerate them in disproportionate numbers in prisons wherein various kinds of forced labor directly echo the conditions of slavery itself.

The spiritual and religious elements of racism are perhaps less obvious, but are especially important: since the impulse to self-righteousness often accompanies the impulse to greed, it has been convenient for racists to evoke a particular kind of hierarchical social system that is supposed to be divinely inspired, in which the basic humanity of Blacks could be diminished—even annihilated—in order to justify the construction of a profoundly exploitative racist society. At the time that the slave trade began to flourish, longstanding arguments had already existed in defense of a divinely sanctioned hierarchy of subordination—of Providence creating (or permitting) social inequality in order to maintain civil peace and order. As Jacob Viner has noted in *The Role of Providence in the Social Order*, in the eighteenth century it was sometimes noted that "God had dealt out his revelations partially, bestowing them on some but not on other peoples, and on some but not on other individuals."[1] This supposedly God-willed inequality was in line with the idea of the Great Chain of Being, which grew out of Aristotle's *Historia animalium*, in which the Greek philosopher ranked animals over plants because they were able to move and sense, and ranked the animals amongst themselves by the nature of their reproductive modes and their blood. Although Aristotle's concept of higher and lower organisms was nonreligious, it was later taken up to form the basis of the medieval Christian idea of the Scala Naturae, which begins with God at its apex and moves down, from angels to humans, from humans to animals, from animals to plants and finally to minerals.

Hierarchies existed within each category of the Chain of Being, including the human, thus allowing for the religiously sanctioned belief in the inferiority of certain people, based on some combination of their social standing, religion, or race. And after the European powers began to explore and then exploit both sub-Saharan Africa and the New World of the Western Hemisphere (both around the same time, in the late fifteenth century), large supplies of cheap labor became increasingly necessary to produce crops such as sugar cane, cotton, and tobacco, which were hugely lucrative and also extremely labor intensive. And as these enterprises grew, in order to justify the merciless, often inhuman, treatment of the people engaged in doing the work, the righteous people who owned those slaves—and what person does not want to be considered righteous?—could justify the social order of slave culture by creating a number of stereotypes that diminished, and even annihilated, the very humanity of the workers they enslaved. As Lisa Farrington makes clear in this book, denying the personhood of a human being lies at the very core of racism. In the case of Africans, this was made palatable to self-righteous White racists by emphasizing the role of inferiority that Providence had assigned to these African "savages," which justified denying them any civil rights, completely excluding them from the body politic and the social fabric of society, and even denying them the right to learn to read and write (uniquely human skills that were prohibited by law in most of the slave states), as well as deeming Africans in general as people "without history."

This notion of Africans having no history, which Lisa Farrington elegantly refutes in this book, is especially evident in the way certain historical and mythological figures are represented in paintings. It was not until I read this book, with its emphasis on painted representations of historical and mythological themes, that I became fully conscious of the degree to which the African origins of so many famous figures from the ancient world have been overlooked or even actively suppressed in modern times and the ways in which they have been culturally "whitewashed." That this is the case may be perceived only implicitly in written texts, but is made quite explicit in visual imagery (including movies). I was especially struck by Farrington's discussion of the story of Andromeda, the remarkably beautiful young princess who is rescued from a sea monster by Zeus's son Perseus. Although I have written at some length about Henri Matisse's references to Andromeda in his sculpture and in one of his major paintings, frankly I had not registered the fact that she was an Ethiopian woman—a Black woman. For as Farrington points out, in Western art this regal and beautiful Black woman who married the godlike Perseus and became the queen of the powerful citadel of Mycenae, is constantly represented as white—even as lily-white (see Farrington's discussion in her essay of figs. 9–13). And as Farrington further points out, the fact that such prominent presences in Western culture as Parzival's brother Feirefiz and the legendary patriarch Prester John, were also Black is often overlooked, as is the Queen of Sheba; how slight is the attention we usually give to the verse in the Song of Solomon: "I am black and comely, oh ye daughters of Jerusalem" (see discussion, p. 50; images pp. 17, 36, 50). To which one might add Cleopatra, Queen of Egypt, who clearly didn't look a bit like Claudette Colbert (1934), Vivien Leigh (1945), or Elizabeth Taylor (1963). Nor, I might add, did the fair-haired, blue-eyed

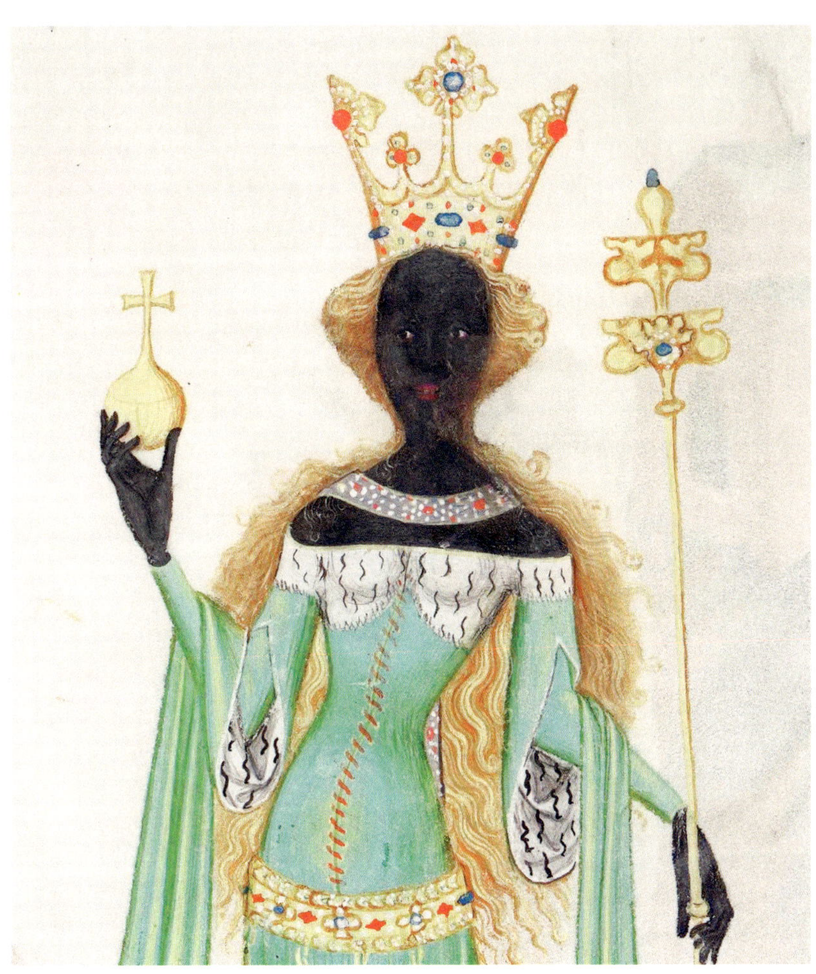

Detail of *Queen of Sheba*, p. 36

young man depicted in the pictures of Jesus sold by Woolworth's when I was a child look at all like the real Jesus Christ.

An important theme that runs throughout this book is the negation of centuries of African history, since negating a people's history is a way of negating their humanity. In its extreme form, this was a view held by polygenists, such as the British-born Jamaican planter Edward Long, who in his 1774 *History of Jamaica* claimed that the White race was a different species than the Black race, and that Black people were not separable from orangutans. And of course, because Long could consider the enslaved people who worked on his plantation to be like animals, he felt morally justified in his belief that that they were the "natural property" of their master, willed to be such by Providence.

An especially telling example of the erasure of African history can be seen in the attitudes that were expressed when the stone walls of Great Zimbabwe came to light during the late nineteenth century. Although it was acknowledged that this magnificent complex had served as the capital of the

Kingdom of Zimbabwe, and had been occupied from the twelfth century until it was abandoned in the mid-fifteenth century, Europeans for a long time denied that such a splendid architectural monument could have actually been built by Africans, proposing instead that the impressive dry-stone masonry had been constructed by Phoenicians or Arabs—anyone but Africans. In the late nineteenth century, Cecil Rhodes had the site torn apart and plundered. In the twentieth century, it was still widely believed, even by some archaeologists, that Africans could not have been capable of building it. In fact, between 1965 and 1980, when the exclusively White Rhodesian Front Party was in power, information about Great Zimbabwe attesting to its construction by Africans was strictly censored in order to reinforce the idea that Africans had no cultural sophistication and no history. The distinguished archaeologist Paul Sinclair later wrote that this was the first time since the days of Nazi Germany that archaeology had been so directly censored.

Lisa Farrington's discussion of the origins and persistence of such attitudes is especially eye-opening. The reader will be surprised to learn that even distinguished philosophers, such as Georg Wilhelm Friedrich Hegel and David Hume, subscribed to intensely racist views (Hume wrote that "there never was a civilized nation of any other complexion than White"),[2] that even such well-known scientists as Linnaeus, Georges Cuvier, Georges-Louis Leclerc de Buffon, and Herbert Spencer (who coined the phrase "survival of the fittest") allowed their racial prejudices to blind them to scientific facts. The reader will also discover that Henry Morton Stanley more or less fabricated his famous story about meeting "Dr. Livingstone, I presume" deep in the wilds of "the Dark Continent."

And I for one was astonished to find the answer to a question I have asked myself almost my whole life, which I have wondered about every time I was asked to fill out a form that asked me to list my race: Why was the racial category to which I was supposed to belong called "Caucasian"? Among the many treasures that this book has to offer is the surprising answer to that question, and many others.

New York, NY
2024

NOTES

1. Jacob Viner, *The Role of Providence in the Social Order: An Essay in Intellectual History* (Princeton: Princeton University Press, 1977), 90.

2. David Hume, "Of National Characters" (1777; revised version of an essay first published 1748).

The World Before Racism

AN ART STORY

LISA E. FARRINGTON, PhD

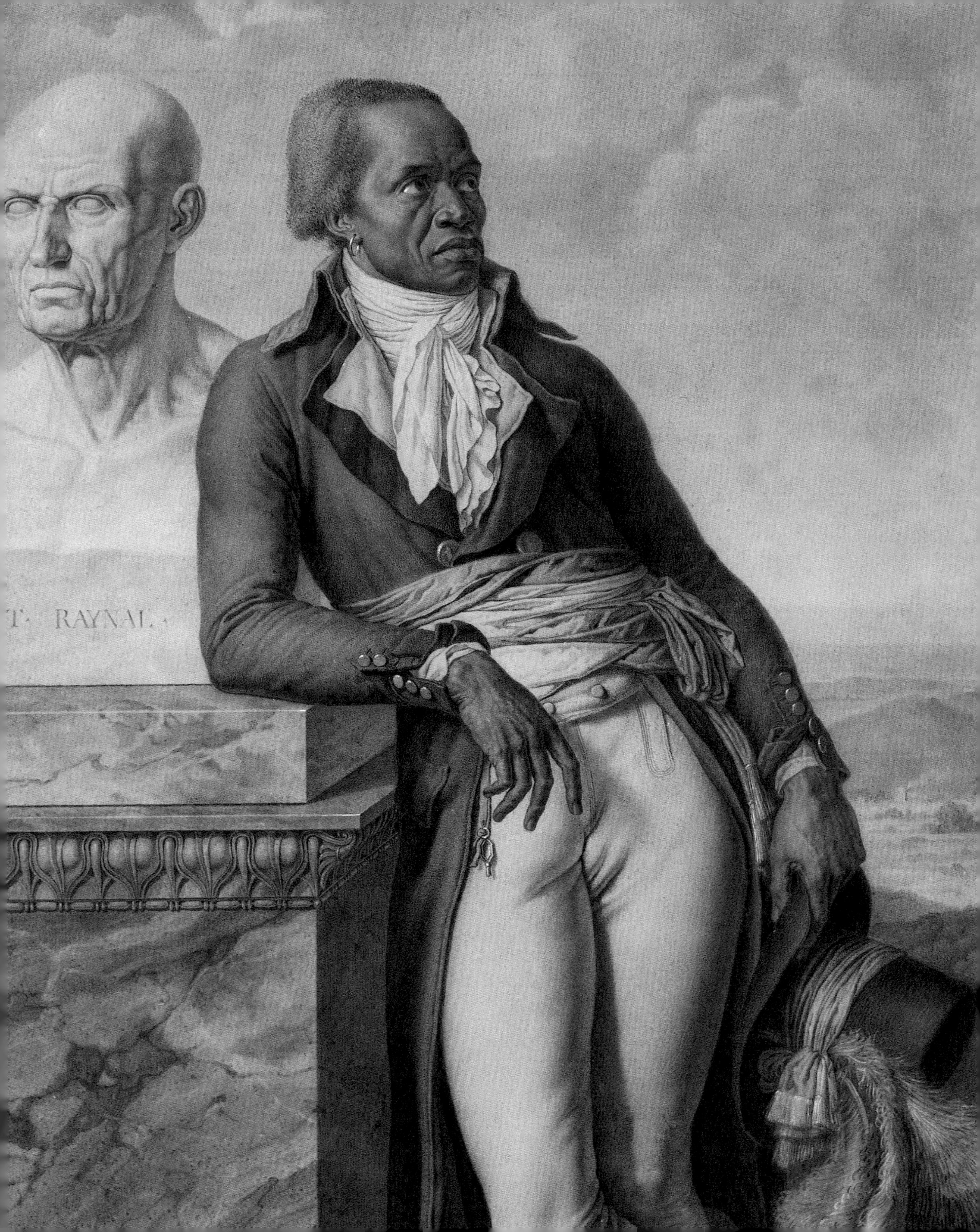
T. RAYNAL

Part One

Art as a Primary Source

Attributed to Anne-Louis Girodet de Roucy-Trioson, *Jean-Baptiste Belley*, ca. 1797
Black chalk, with stumping, and traces of pen and black ink, heightened with touches of opaque white, on ivory wove paper
14 9/16 × 11 15/16 in. (36.9 × 30.3 cm)
Purchased with funds provided by the Joseph and Helen Regenstein Foundation
The Art Institute of Chicago; acc. no. 1973.156

Despite evident strides in the direction of racial harmony, we continue to live in a racially charged world plagued by xenophobic fears, misunderstandings, and stereotypes. The most palpable of stereotypes for people of African descent are criminality and moral and mental inferiority—misperceptions that doggedly pursue Blacks no matter how outstanding their achievements or how far they move beyond the age when these myths were first invented. Even someone as highly regarded as former President Obama—who has been the butt of numerous racist slurs—is not exempt. This brings us to several important questions: When did racism begin? Who started it? Has the well-worn antagonism between Blacks and Whites always existed? Or is this a relatively new phenomenon?

A way to most effectively ferret out the answers to these questions is to consult primary-source documents. A primary-source document is one that is uniquely and reliably representative of the belief systems of a particular age and culture because it was produced by the people of that age and culture. Examples of primary sources include original plays, codified law, letters, interviews, and of course, visual art. As unmodified and unfiltered "texts" (any objects or documents that communicate information), primary sources have the potential to provide the most accurate and direct information about the people who produced them. Primary sources stand in stark contrast to secondary ones that alter, adulterate, extract from, expand upon, or in some way modify the primary source. This gives the visual arts a distinct advantage over the written word—an advantage that lies in the fact that art, by nature, is almost always a primary source, existing principally in its original form.

The written word is far less reliable than visual art because it is vulnerable to alteration when we must translate original (primary) written documents from one language to another; or rewrite them using modern vernacular if the texts are antique. Adding to the difficulty in accurately reading written works is that, in their original form, writings are often rare and inaccessible due to the fragility of their format, such as with an antique book or scroll that must be preserved in near-hermetic humidity- and light-controlled environments. As a result, most of the written texts available to us are reprints or copies. As such, they are secondary sources that may or may not be representative of the originals and may well result in the muddying of the author's intended content and meaning. Similar to the way that a game of "telephone" guarantees that the final player will not have heard the original message, the more "editors" there

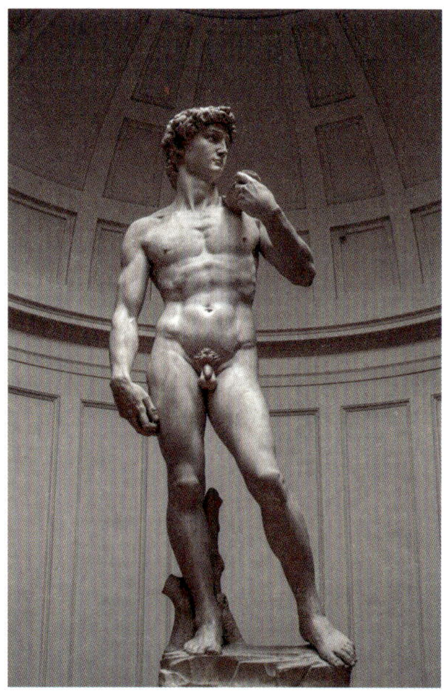

Fig. 1

Michelangelo (Italian, 1475–1564),
David, 1501–1504
Carrara marble
14 3⁄16 x 78 5⁄16 in. (434 x 199 cm)
Galleria dell'Accademia, Florence, Italy;
acc. no. 1076

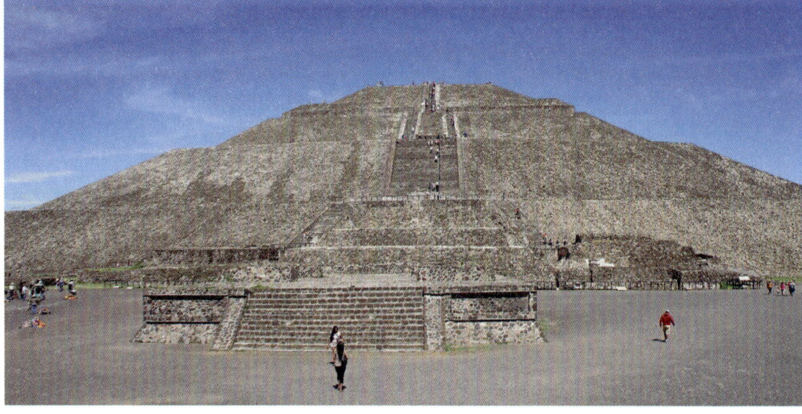

Fig. 2

Pyramid of the Sun at Teotihuacan,
Anahuac, Mexico, ca. 200 CE
Basalt blocks, lime plaster, and paint
215 x 720 x 735 ft.
(65.5 x 220 x 224 m)
Toltec culture, Miccaotli period
(UNESCO World Heritage List, 1987)

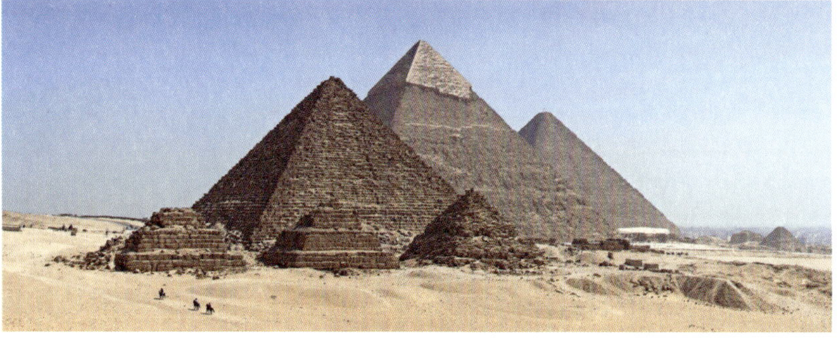

Fig. 3

Great Pyramids at Giza, Egypt, ca.
2600–2500 BCE, Fourth Dynasty of
the Old Kingdom
Granite and limestone blocks, mortar,
and limestone plaster
Great Pyramid (Pyramid of Khufu):
481 ft. high x 750 ft. square (146.6 x
228.6 m)
Pyramid of Khafre: 450 ft. high x
695 ft. square (137.2 x 211.8 m)
Pyramid of Menkaure: 200 ft. high x
356 ft. square (61 x 108.5 m)

Fig. 4

BELOW, LEFT

Olmec Head, ca. 1200–900 BCE
Basalt
9 13⁄16 ft. high × 14 3⁄4 ft. in circumference (3 × 4.5 m)
Collection of the Xalapa Museo de Antropologia de Xalapa, Xalapa, Vera Cruz, Mexico
Image source: https://smarthistory.org/olmec-colossal-heads/

Fig. 5

BELOW, RIGHT

Charles K. Wilkinson, *Nubian Tribute Presented to the King*, ca. 1923–1927 (detail)
Tempera on paper
71 5⁄8 in. × 206 5⁄16 in. (182 × 524 cm)
Wall paintings from Tomb of Huy, Viceroy of Nubia buried at Qurnat Murai, New Kingdom, Dynasty 18, reigns of Thutmose IV and Amenhotep III, 1353–1327 BCE, Thebes, Upper Egypt
Metropolitan Museum of Art, New York, NY, Rogers Fund, 1930; acc. no. 30.4.21

are of a given text, the more its original meaning is distorted. Take the New Testament, for example, which within two generations of Christ's death produced no fewer than four versions by Saints Matthew, Mark, Luke, and John. Seen in this light, art often proves to be a more direct link to accurate information about both the makers of the art and their cultural and historical milieu. Furthermore, as will be demonstrated in the section of this book that discusses Charles Darwin, secondary sources, if widely read and believed, can be detrimental to our understanding of the past and, thus, to our beliefs in the present.

While the written word is vulnerable to an endless array of editing, visual art never appears in translation. It begins and ends as a primary source of information. Visual-art objects are neither reinterpretations nor reconfigurations. They are available for study in their original form, such as Anne-Louis Girodet de Roussy-Trioson's portrait of J. B. Belley (p. 20). Unlike the written word, a masterpiece by Michelangelo doesn't need to be resculpted for the sake of modern interpretation. It exists the same today as it did when it was carved over five hundred years ago (fig. 1). The architectural and engineering feats of the pre-Columbian and Egyptian pyramid builders cannot be denied because their monuments stand unaltered (figs. 2, 3). We need not wonder what the Olmecs, the founding fathers of ancient Mexico, perceived as ideal and noble beauty—their faces remain as they fashioned them some 3,000 years ago (fig. 4). Nor do we have to guess as to the existence of ancient Nubian royalty or their diplomatic relations with Egypt—their images haunt us from the walls of Egyptian tombs (fig. 5). That Egyptian culture honored Nubian warriors as some of the finest military men of the ancient world is evident in venerable wooden figures carved by Egyptian royal sculptors (fig. 6).

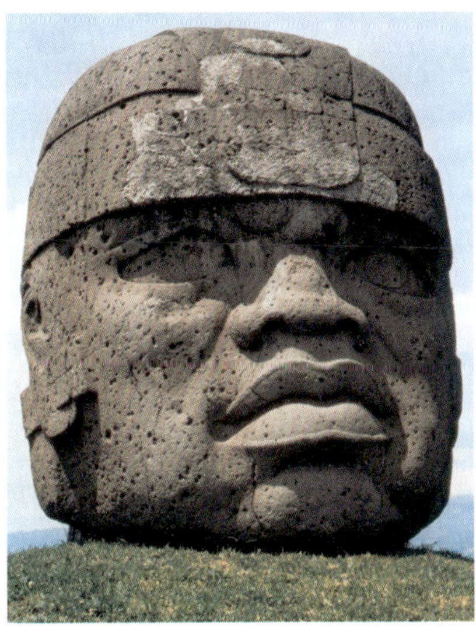

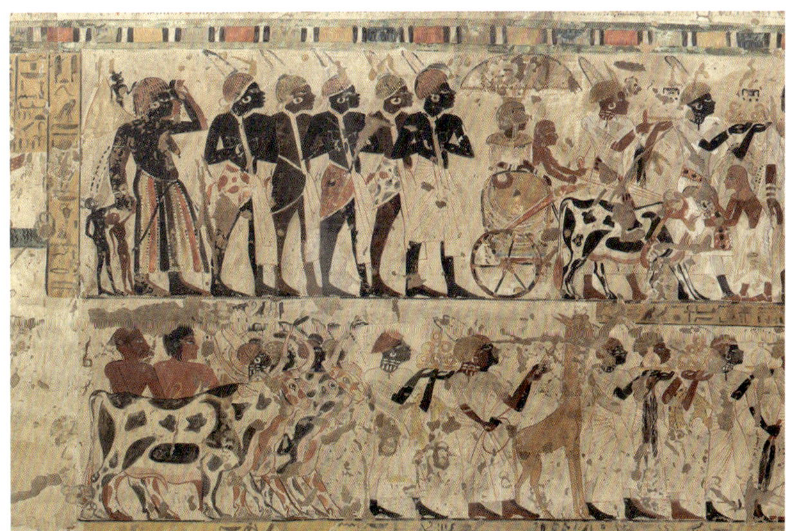

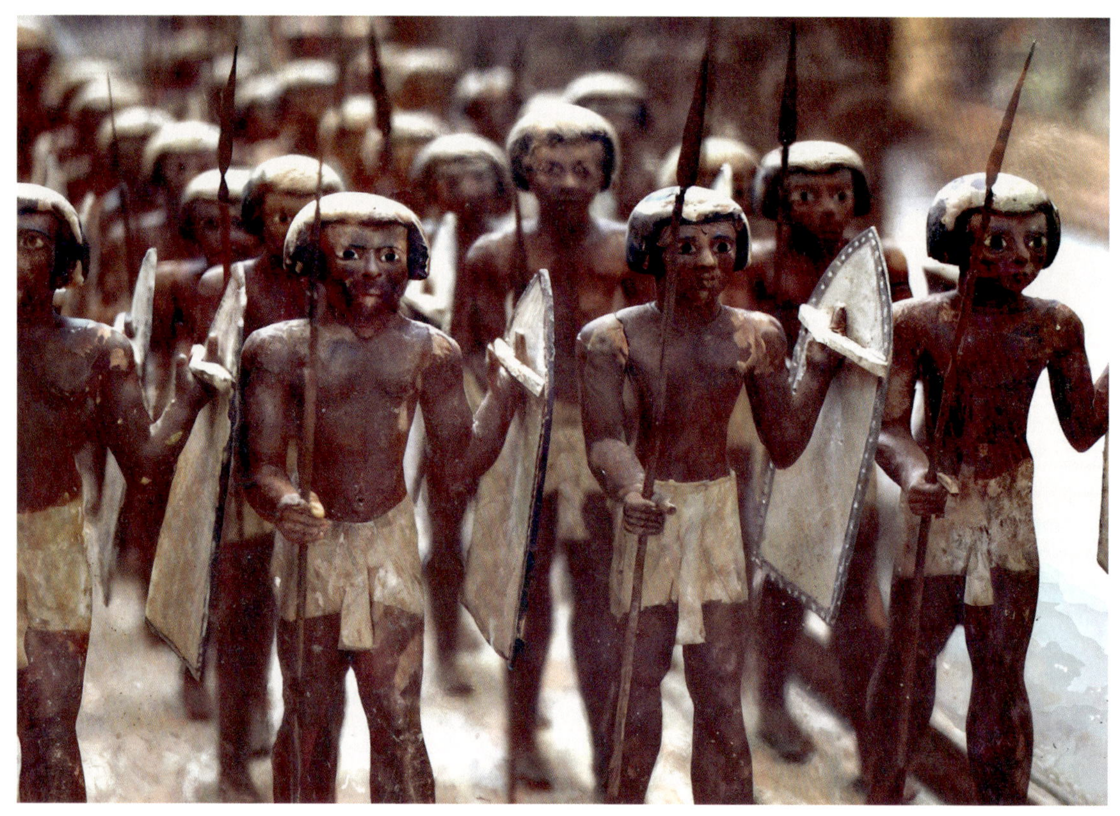

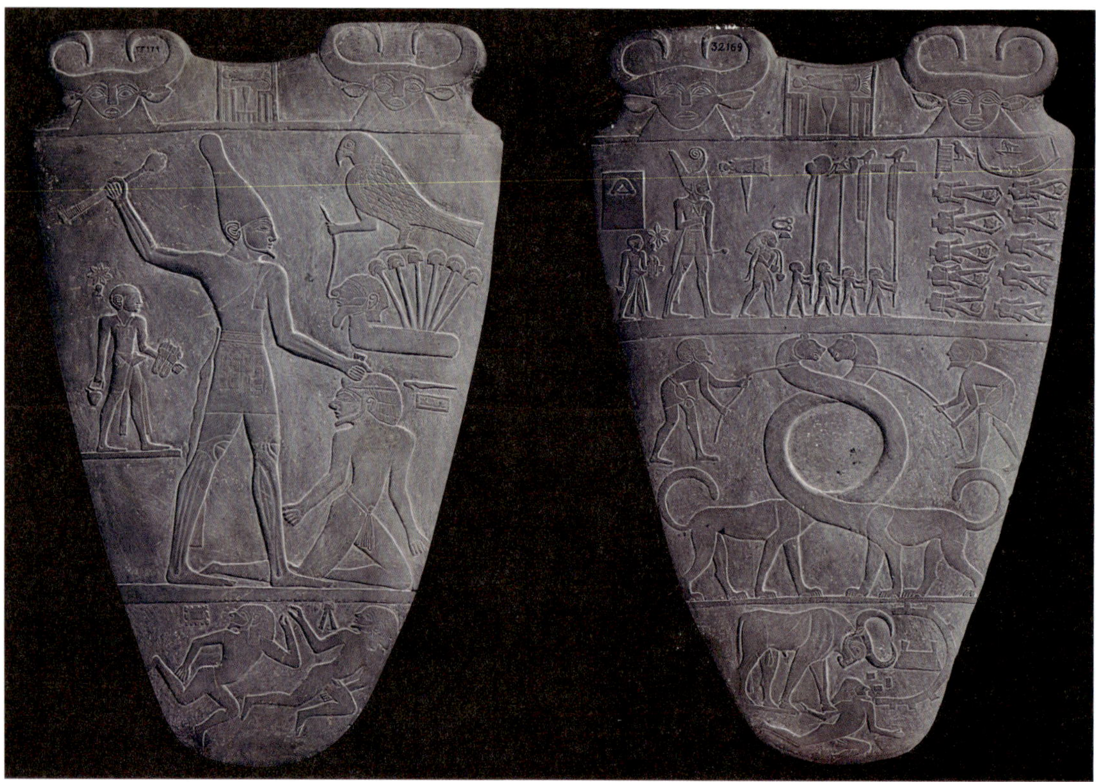
32169

Fig. 6

OPPOSITE, TOP

Troop of Nubian warriors from the Tomb of Prince Mesehti at Assyut
Painted wood
Egyptian Middle Kingdom, 11th Dynasty, 2061–2010 BCE
The Egyptian National Museum, Cairo, Egypt, Photograph: Udimu

Fig. 7

OPPOSITE, BOTTOM

Palette of Narmer, 3200–3000 BCE
Siltstone
25 3/16 x 16 1/2 in. (64 x 42 cm)
The Egyptian Museum, Cairo, Egypt, CG 14716

Visual art is a much more accurate indicator of cultural perceptions than secondary-source literature. To accurately interpret works of art, one must be visually literate. As the phrase suggests, visual literacy describes the ability to "read" images as one might read words; that is, to understand how images communicate and what they are saying. Art, as a nuanced and complex visual language, has the potential to speak volumes about the history, experiences, culture, and philosophies of artists, patrons, and the societies that fostered them. Indeed, in many cases, art provides as much, if not more information about human history than written language. What we know about ancient Egyptian society, religion, politics, and history, for example, is imparted to us through architectural monuments such as pyramids and temples, and through sculpture and hieroglyphics, a language of icons that formed the basis for later alphabets. The same can be said of ancient Greece, a culture about which we have gleaned much from its visual art and architecture, such as knowledge of its ideals of human beauty or the importance of its Olympic games. Indeed, historians routinely study works of art in order to best understand a given time, place, and ethos.

The Ancient World

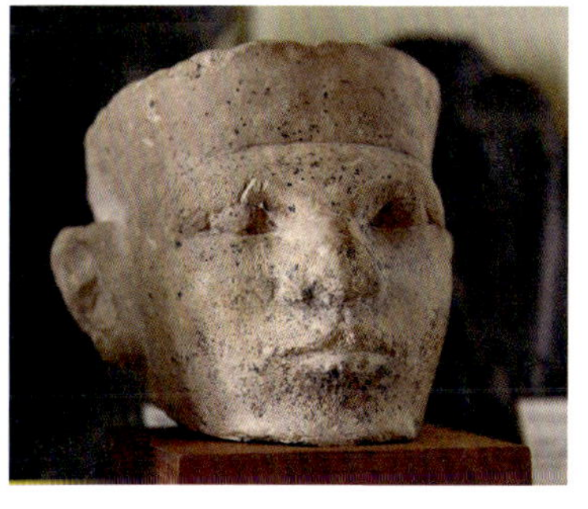

Fig. 8

Head of Narmer, 3100–2850 BCE, pharaoh of Egypt's first dynasty and first unifier of Upper and Lower Egypt
Limestone
4 7/8 x 31 5/16 in. (12.3 x 10 cm)
The Petrie Museum of Egyptian Archaeology, London, UK
Acc. no. LDUCE-UC15989
Photograph courtesy of Wikimedia Commons

Beginning with European economic and military ascendancy following the Renaissance, the configuration of Western history began to shroud even the immutable truths told by art objects, and it has done so by virtue of omission. If certain images are simply excluded from educational texts or kept in museum storage areas rather than on display, the result is the same as that of a rewritten book: truth is altered, veiled or, as is the case with so much African history, quite literally erased. Take, for example, the well-known *Palette of Narmer* (fig. 7), reproduced in virtually every major art survey textbook published in the United States in the twentieth century. It documents the historic formation of the great ancient Egyptian empire by the first pharaohs. Yet, the palette does not offer us a look at the faces of those pharaohs, who some past scholars have insisted were European rather than African (fig. 8).[1] Not that portraits of the early Egyptian rulers are unavailable to us; on the contrary, they are simply rarely reproduced or displayed.[2]

Fortunately, primary-source documents about Africans, whether they are works of art or original manuscripts, have doggedly survived the passage of time, allowing for the present-day historian/detective to reconstruct the facts of African existence with amazing fidelity and to offer a very different history of Africans than the one to which most of us have access.[3] This book is unique because the primary sources utilized herein were, by and large, produced by Europeans and, therefore, express the attitudes and opinions that Europeans had about Africans over the millennia and before the modern age—attitudes that bear little resemblance to those of this current era. For example, both sculptural and literary primary sources from ancient Greece indicate that the cultures of Africans or Ethiopians (from the original Greek words for "land of color," *a-phrike*; and the word for Sudan and sub-Saharan Africa—*Aethiopia* or "burnt face")[4] were considered to be among the world's elites, ranked by the Greeks themselves as even superior to Hellenic culture.

In Homer's eighth-century-BCE epic, *Odyssey*, Odysseus's herald Eurybates of Ithaca was described as follows: "He was round-shouldered, dark-skinned, and woolly-haired, and Odysseus honored him above all his other comrades."[5] The Greek historian Diodorus (Siculus—from Sicily), who lived between 30 and 90 BCE, wrote in his *Histories* as did Homer in his *Iliad*, "For Zeus had yesterday to Ocean's bounds set forth to feast with Africa's faultless men, and he was followed there by all the gods"—faultless Africans, as in perfect, without error, and the preferred company of the gods of Olympus.[6] Vitruvius, the first-century-BCE Roman author, wrote in book 6 of his *On Architecture*, "The African nations are quick in understanding and intelligent with good judgment." On the other hand, Northern Europeans are "more courageous in war and fearlessly attacked their enemies, [but do so] without consideration or judgment [and are thus unsuccessful in their military campaigns]."[7] In other words, Europeans were considered the brawn and Africans the brains in the first century BCE.

In classical mythology, Africans were honored by Ovid in the tale of Andromeda—a chaste and beautiful Black princess who was the daughter of King Cepheus and Queen Cassiopeia of Africa.[8] After the Queen insulted Poseidon's sea nymphs (the Nereids) by claiming that both she and her daughter were more beautiful than they, Poseidon punished them by sending the sea monster, Cetus, to destroy their kingdom. To save themselves, the king and queen offered their daughter up as a sacrifice to Cetus; and chained her to a rock at the ocean's edge to await the demon's wrath. Just at this moment, the Greek hero Perseus flew overhead on his winged horse Pegasus. He was returning home to Greece after decapitating the snake-headed Gorgon, Medusa, and he was overwhelmed by Andromeda's beauty:

> Till Aethiopia's shore appear'd at last.
> Andromeda was there, doom'd to attone
> By her own ruin follies not her own . . .
> Chain'd to a rock she stood; young Perseus stay'd
> His rapid flight, to view the beauteous maid.
> So sweet her frame, so exquisitely fine,
> She seem'd a statue by a hand divine,
> Had not the wind her waving tresses show'd,

And down her cheeks the melting sorrows flow'd.
Her faultless form the heroe's bosom fires;
The more he looks, the more he still admires.
Th' admirer almost had forgot to fly,
And swift descended, flutt'ring from on high.
O! Virgin, worthy no such chains to prove,
But pleasing chains in the soft folds of love . . . [9]

Using the snake-encrusted Gorgon's head, Perseus turned the sea monster into stone and saved Andromeda. He eventually married her—entering into an interracial union in which Perseus decidedly married up (fig. 9). Evidence of the ancient world's racially hybrid nature and of the fact that the ancients did not perceive African features as a negative can be seen in vase paintings that depict Andromeda and her retinue with either cropped curly hair or round noses. It is important to note that antiquity was a world of mixed

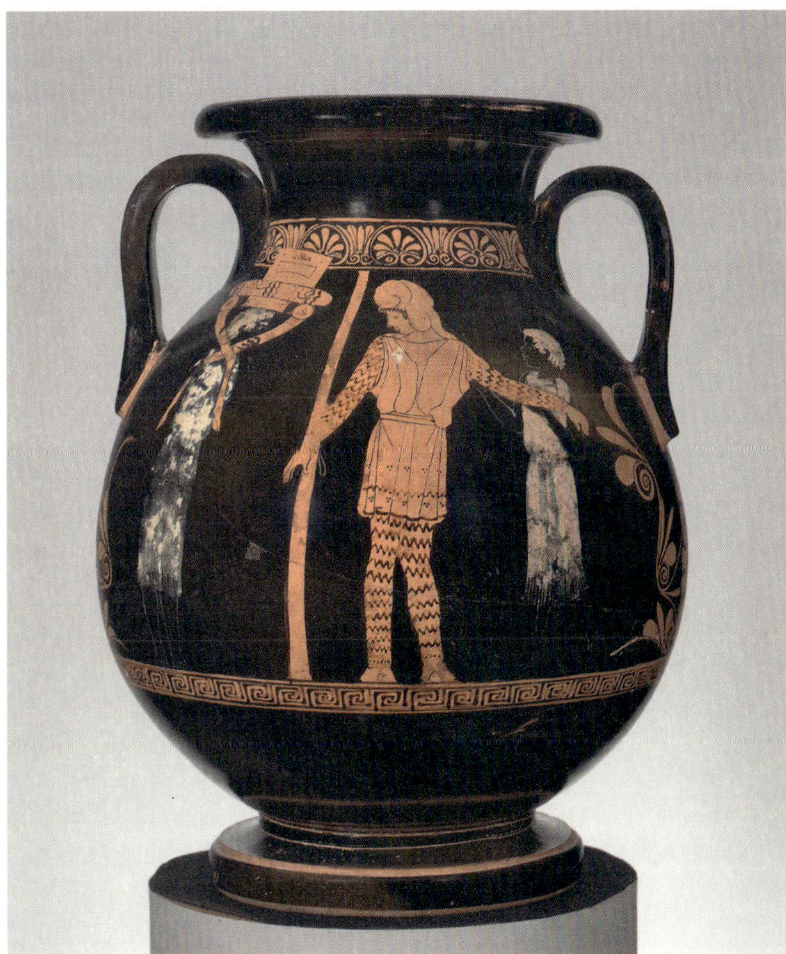

Fig. 9

Workshop of the Niobid Painter, *Pelike* (detail of Andromeda), Greek Classical Period, 450–440 BCE
Ceramic red figure vase
17 5/16 x 12 5/8 in. (44 x 32.1 cm)
Museum of Fine Arts, Boston, Boston, MA
Arthur Tracy Cabot Fund; acc. no. 63.2663
Photograph © 2024, Museum of Fine Arts, Boston

ethnicities and skin color, per se, did not play a major role in determining status.[10] For example, Kushites (ancient Nubians), who occupied the area south of Egypt, are referred to in the Hebrew Bible as a powerful and wealthy nation comprised of tall and beautiful people with Black skin, and Moses is said to have married a Kushite woman.[11]

Antiquity was often marked by an appreciation of dark beauty as opposed to more recent centuries wherein European beauty has been held in high esteem. Not surprisingly, in recent history, there ceases to be any reference to the African heritage of Andromeda, evident in well-known paintings on the subject by nineteenth-century Symbolist artist Gustave Moreau (fig. 10) and by Edward Burne-Jones, both of whom depict Andromeda as distinctly European (fig. 11). In twentieth-century films, Andromeda fares no better. Ignoring Greek primary sources, Hollywood chose to portray the African princess as European in both the 1981 and 2010 movie versions of *Clash of the Titans*, starring respectively Harry Hamlin and Liam Neeson. In 1981, Andromeda was played by the blond-haired British actress Judi Bowker (fig. 12) and in 2010 the French-born actress Alexa Davalos was cast in the role (fig. 13).

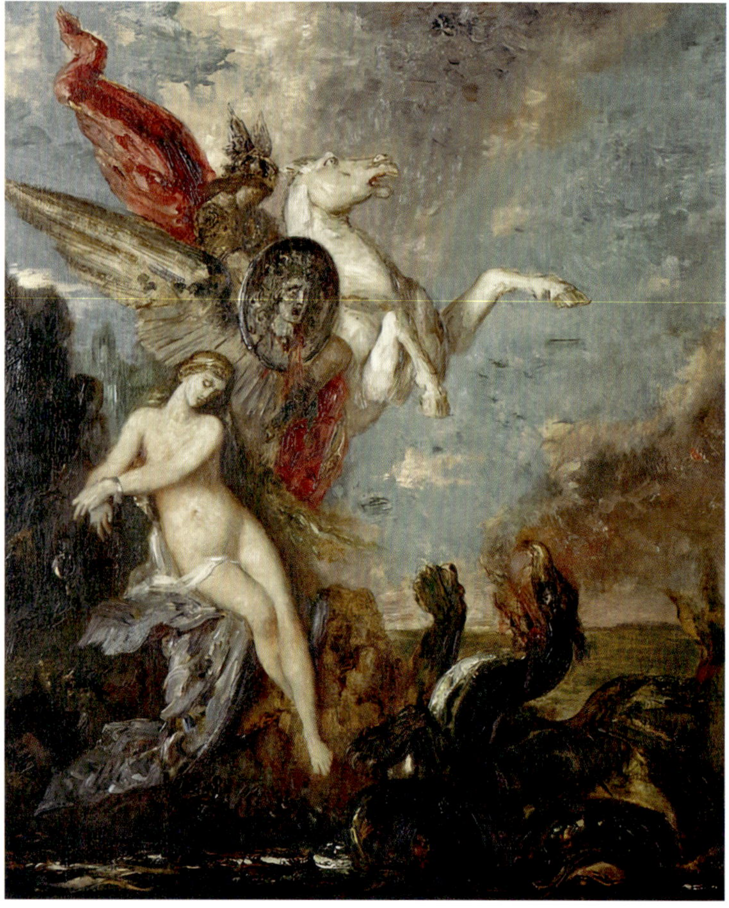

Fig. 10

Gustave Moreau, *Andromeda Chained to a Rock Delivered by Perseus*, ca. 1867–1869
Oil on canvas
21½ x 16¾ in. (54.6 x 42.5 cm)
Collection of the Musée Gustave Moreau, Paris, France

Fig. 11

Edward Burne-Jones, *The Perseus Series: The Rock of Doom*, 1884–1885
Watercolor
60⅝ x 50⅝ in. (154 x 128.6 cm)
Collection of the Southampton City Art Gallery, Southhampton, UK

Fig. 12

BOTTOM, LEFT

Harry Hamlin and Judi Bowker, *Clash of the Titans*, 1981
Directed By Desmond Davis
Medium: Film still
Photograph © Charles H. Schneer Productions/Metro-Goldwyn-Mayer Pictures / Diltz / Bridgeman Images

Fig. 13

BOTTOM, RIGHT

Alexa Davalos, *Clash of the Titans,* 2010
AJ Pics / Alamy Stock Photo

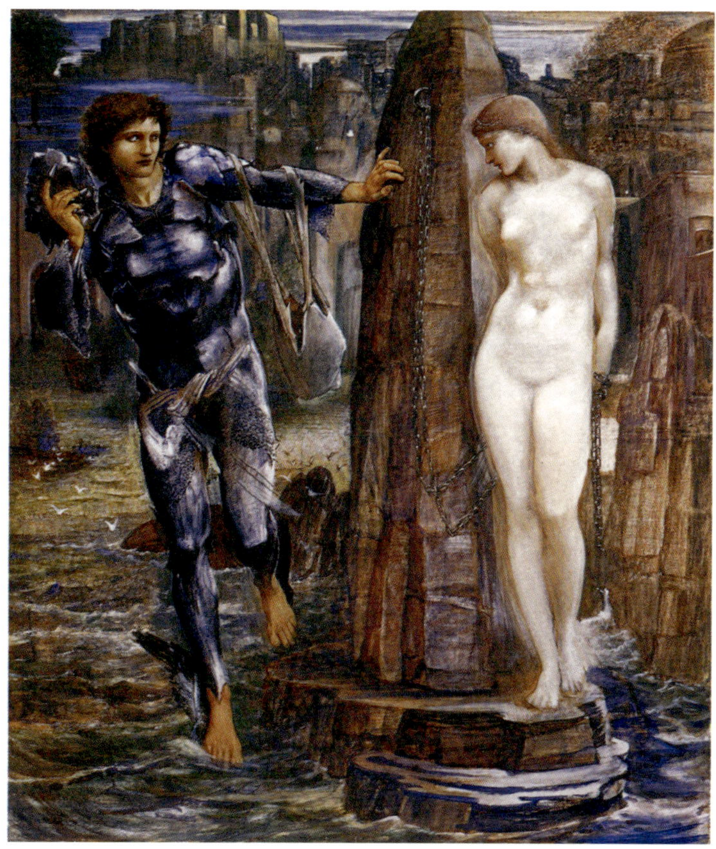

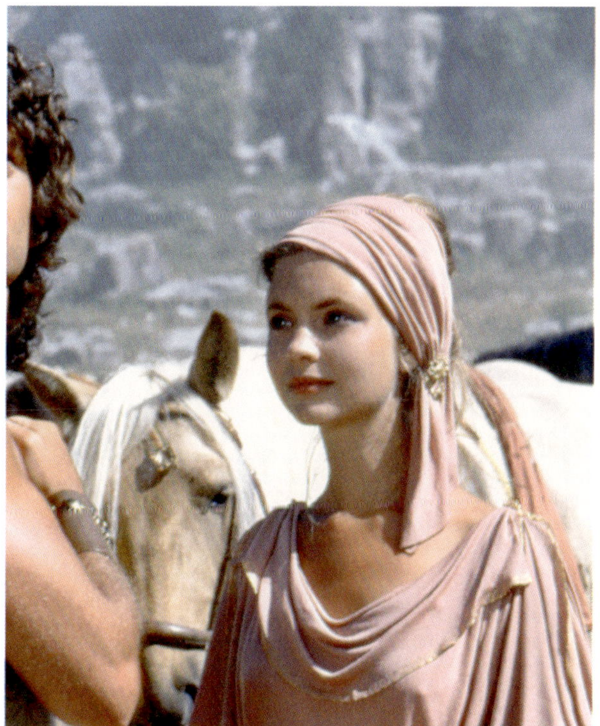

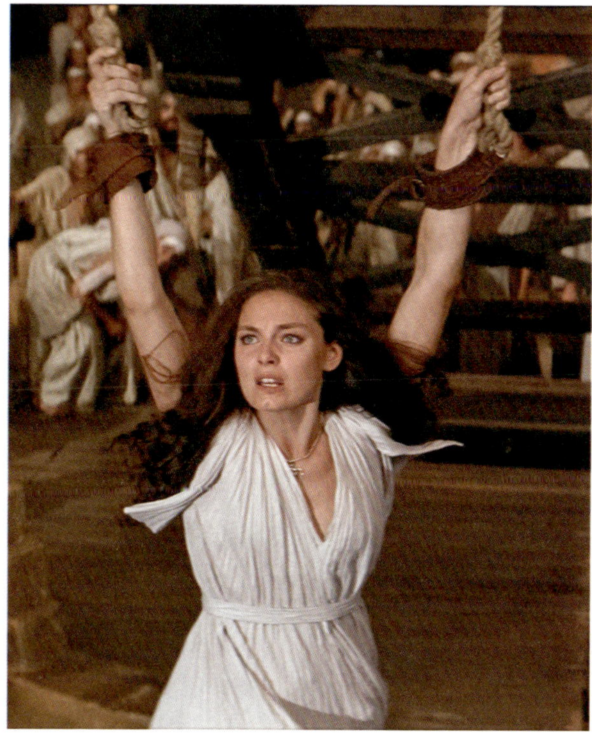

Sadly, movies and television are the sources for much of our so-called knowledge of history today. Greek paintings of Hercules, of Circe the enchantress (fig. 14), and the Nike or winged victory figures were often given African features by the artists who portrayed them in the form of a visual shorthand that included protruding round noses and enlarged mouths (fig. 15). Again, in more recent years these mythical personae have rarely, if ever, been portrayed as Black, as in the 1911 John William Waterhouse painting of the irresistible Circe as a redhead (fig. 16). The ancient Greeks were fascinated with the features of Africans precisely because those features were so unlike their own. Rather than

Fig. 14

Black Circe and Odysseus, Greece, Boeotian, 450–420 BCE
Incised black-figured skyphos vase decorated with the loom of Circe, who is shown with Odysseus and one of his sailors, changed to an animal; excavated from the Cabeirion Sanctuary at Thebes (Luxor); inscribed "KIRKA"
7½ x 7½ in. (19.05 x 19.05 cm)
The British Museum, London, UK; Acc. no. 1893,0303
Photograph courtesy of The British Museum

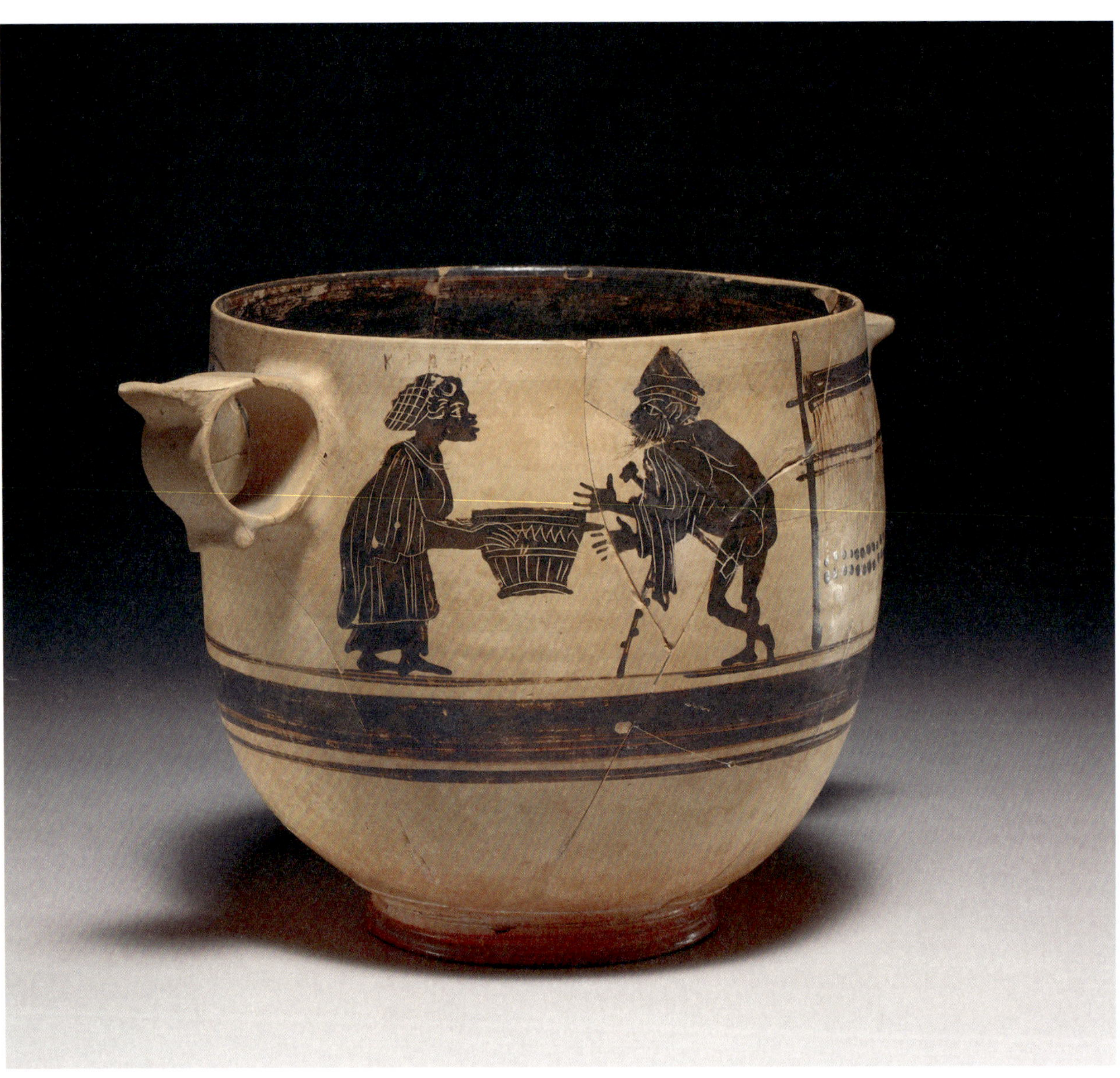

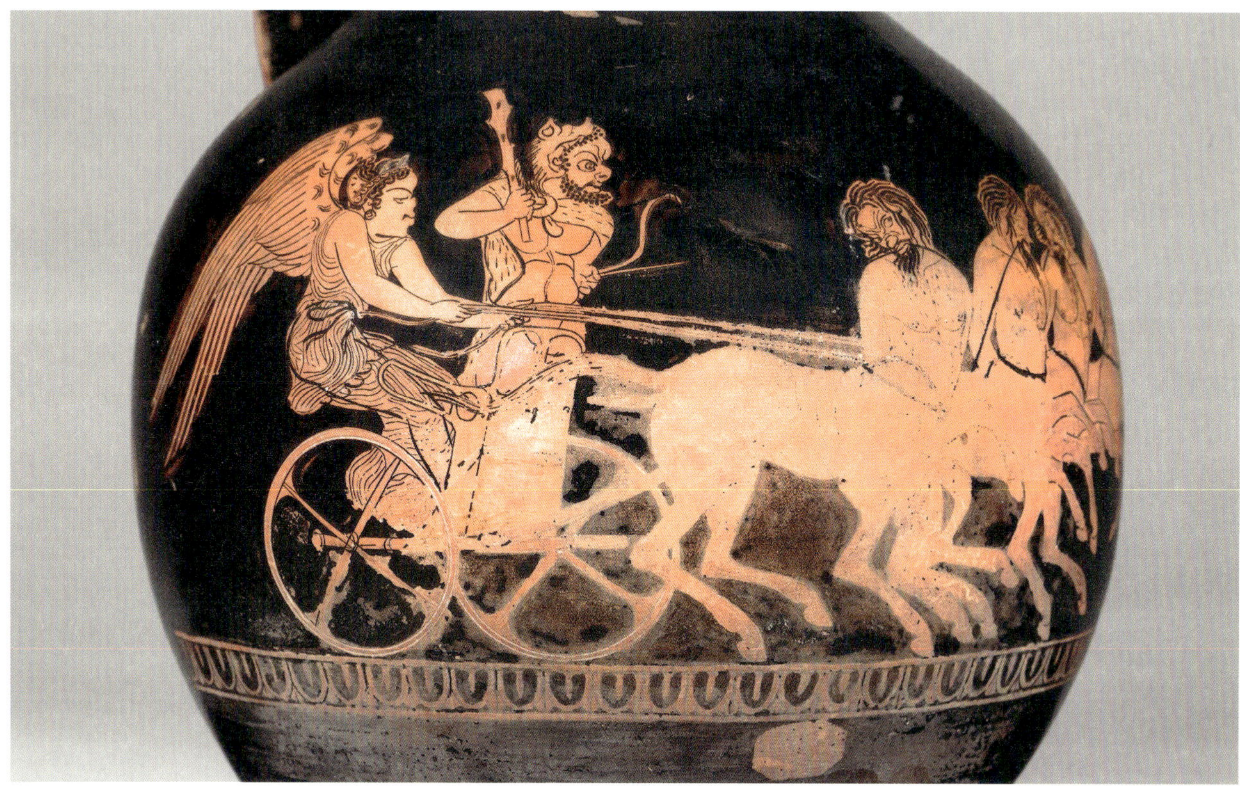

Fig. 15

ABOVE

Attributed to the Nikias Painter, *Black Victory Driving Herakles in Chariot*, ca. 410–400 BCE
Attic red figure vase, terracotta, Oinochoe shape; excavated from Cyrenaica, Greece
8 3⁄4 in. high (22.3 cm)
Musée du Louvre, Paris, France
Catalogue no. Louvre N3408

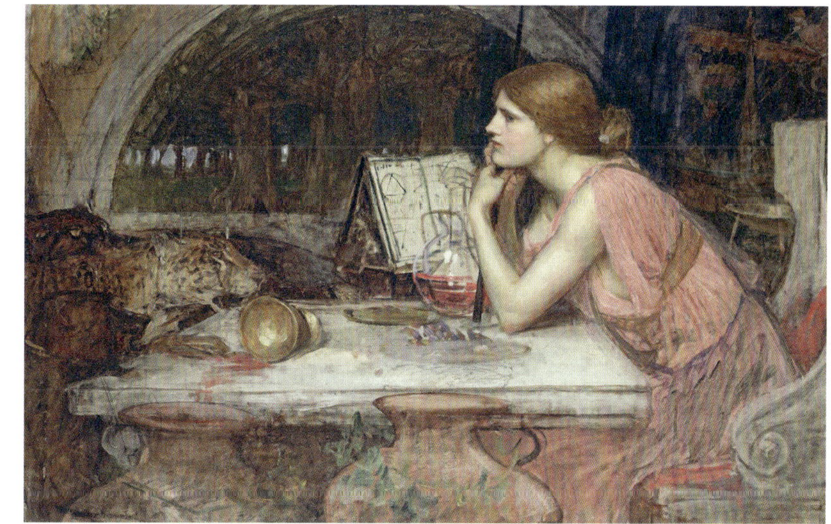

Fig. 16

RIGHT

John William Waterhouse (English, 1849–1917), *Circe (The Sorceress)*, 1911
Oil on canvas
29 15⁄16 x 43 1⁄2 in. (76 x 110.5 cm)
Private collection
Photograph courtesy of Bridgeman Images, Brooklyn, NY

disdaining difference, they embraced it and were quick to appreciate diverse types of human beauty, often depicting this diversity in fifth-century vase painting (fig. 17). Hellenic admiration for African military prowess is also well documented in Greek vase painting by numerous representations of Black warriors (fig. 18) and in repeated depictions of the legendary African, Busiris, who was a priest of the Egyptian god Osiris and who once imprisoned Herakles (or Hercules; fig. 19). More than mere mythology, there exists a Hellenistic bronze sculpture of a model posed as a musician, which allows us to visualize an actual African, conceived by a Greek sculptor as sublimely beautiful and graceful (fig. 20). The ancient Greeks' total comfort level with and acceptance of people unlike themselves, and their complete lack of racial prejudice may well explain, at least in part, why, even today theirs is considered one of the most evolved and sophisticated civilizations in human history.

Fig. 17

LEFT

Herakles and African, ca. 480–470 BCE
Attic Kantharos vase of the Vatican Class M, Vulci, painted ceramic
7 13/16 x 7 7/16 in. (19.8 cm x 18.8 cm)
Collection of the Vatican Museo Gregoriano Etrusco, Vatican City, Italy
Catalogue no. 16539

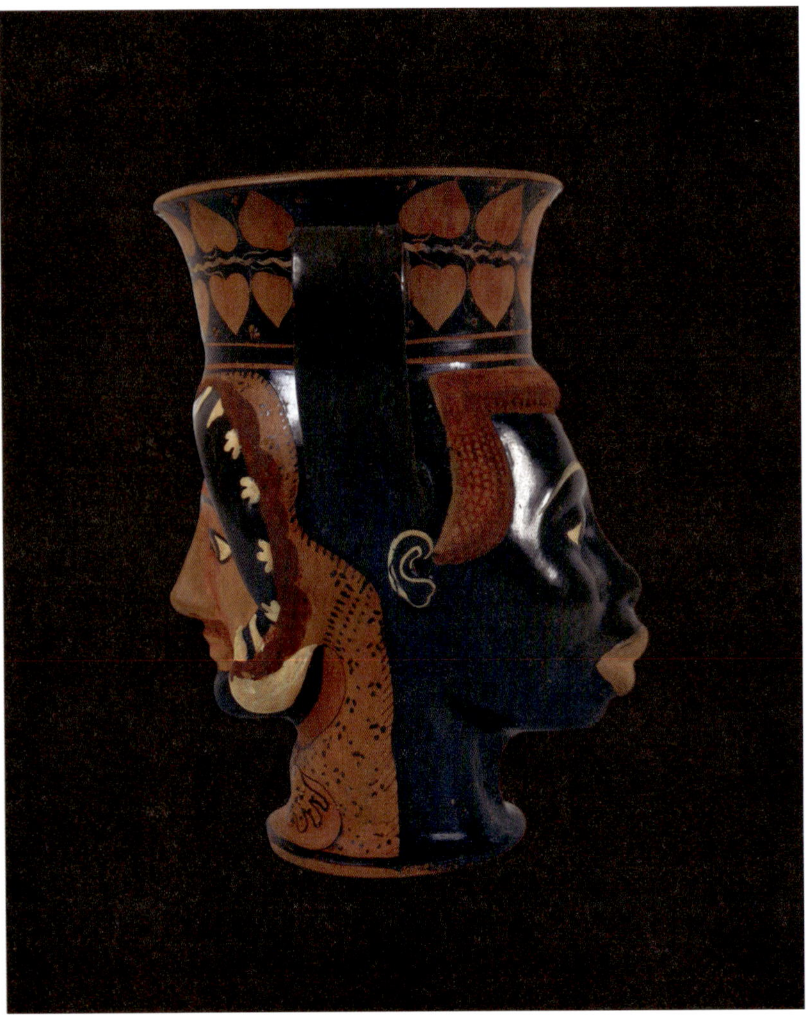

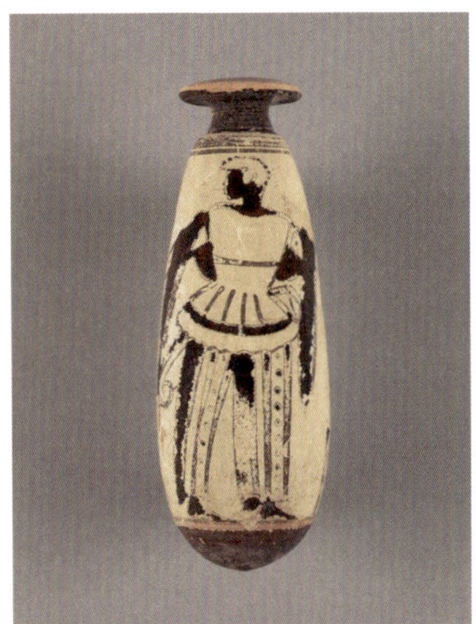

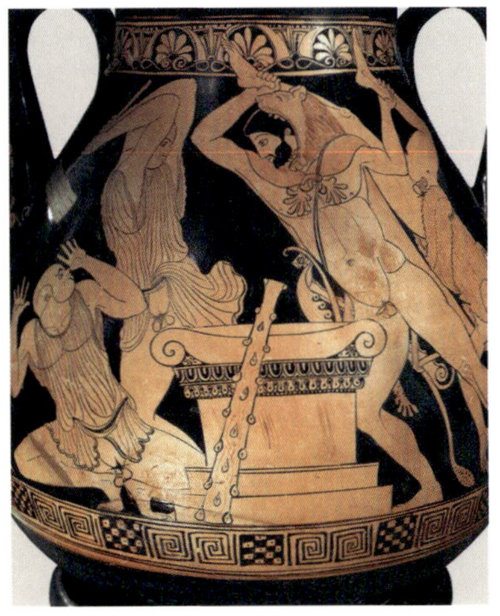

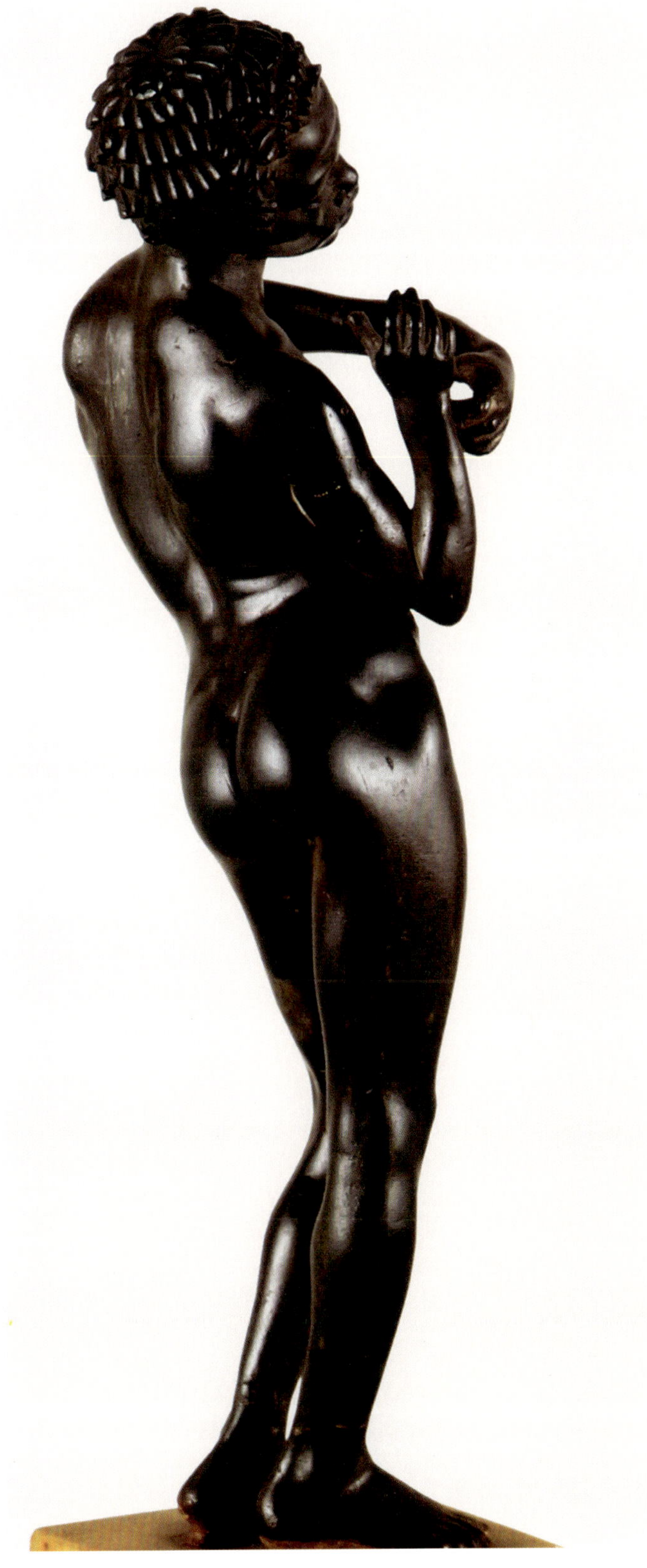

Fig. 18

OPPOSITE, TOP RIGHT

Ethiopian Archer, ca. 480 BCE
White-ground Attic alabastron, terracotta; Athenian Greek
5 11/16 in. high (14.5 cm)
J. Paul Getty Museum, Malibu, CA
Villa Collection; 71.AE.202

Fig. 19

OPPOSITE, BOTTOM RIGHT

Pan Painter (Greek School), *Herakles Overthrowing Busiris*, fifth century BCE
Attic pelike
The National Museum, Athens, Greece
Photograph courtesy of Bridgeman Images, Brooklyn, NY

Fig. 20

RIGHT

Young Nubian Musician from Chalon-sur-Saône, Hellenistic Period, ca. 323–30 BCE, Greece
Bronze
7 15/16 in. high (20.2 cm)
Bibliothèque Nationale, Paris, France

The ancient Romans are not far behind. Sculptures from the time of Christ depict the African citizens of Rome with honor, such as fearsome West African warriors with filed teeth and tightly coiled hair (figs. 21, 22). Venerable portraits of Black Roman dignitaries and senators also still exist, including one of Memnon, the beloved student and adopted son of Greek-born rhetorical philosopher Herodes Atticus, who lived in the Roman Empire from 101–177 CE (figs. 23, 24).[12] African *mahouts*, or highly skilled elephant drivers, drove forty pack elephants over the Alps for Hannibal in the third century BCE to defeat the Romans in the Second Punic War. These Black *mahouts* so impressed the Romans that they were immortalized on Roman coins (fig. 25).

It is evident from these key examples that from its very beginnings, Western civilization was not marred by prejudice based on skin color. Greeks believed that Africans were their moral superiors and closer to ideal beauty than the Greeks themselves, and they were self-assured enough to admit this in their own art and myths. Furthermore, while Greek mythology is mainly available to modern readers in translation, reliable translations are available, but these must be carefully sought out and researched. The same can be said for Roman writings, which reflect the truth observed in their art. Romans, who revered strength and stoicism, were ready to acknowledge in art and literature the skill and prowess of their adversaries, no matter their skin color, and to acknowledge Africans as Roman citizens. This phenomenon of European esteem for Africans was not, however, limited to ancient times, but continued for many centuries.

Fig. 21

BOTTOM, LEFT

Terracotta jug in the shape of a head of a Black African, Imperial Rome, third century CE
Terracotta
7 1/8 in. high (18.1 cm)
The Metropolitan Museum of Art, New York, NY
Gift of J. Pierpont Morgan, 1917; acc. no: 17.194.859

Fig. 22

BOTTOM, RIGHT

Fragment of a balsamarium in the form of a Black male head, late third or early second century BCE
Bronze
3 in. high (7.7 cm)
Current location unknown

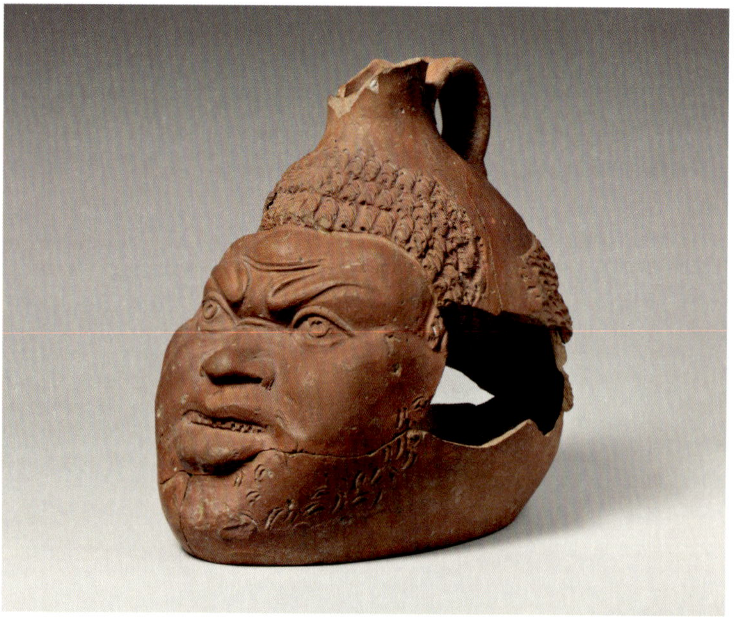

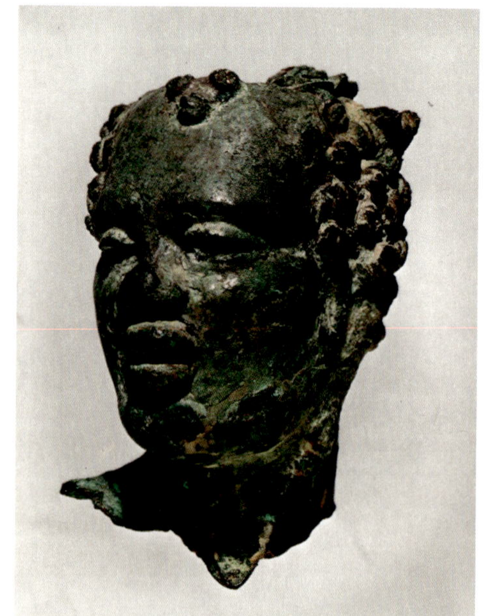

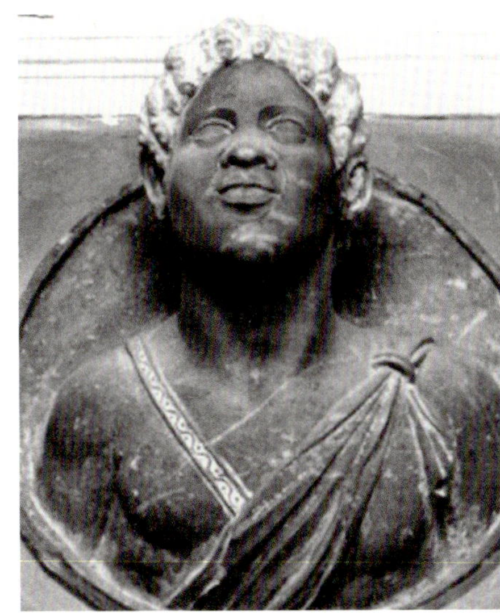

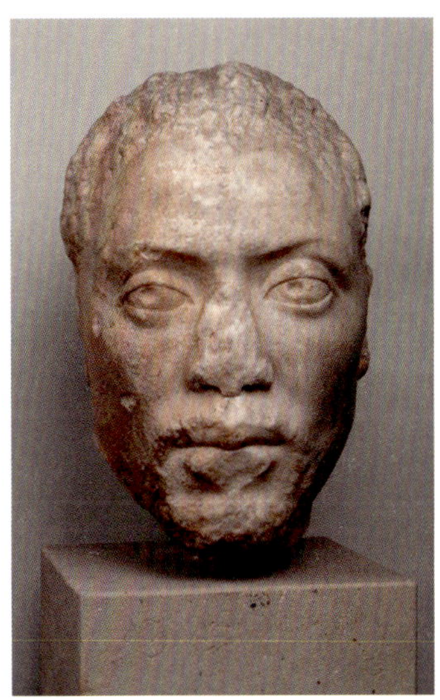

Fig. 23

TOP, LEFT

Bust of Ethiopian, 1st AD
Gray-black marble
55 1/8 in. diameter (140 cm)
Collection of Museo Torlonia, Rome

Fig. 24

TOP, RIGHT

Portrait of Memnon, Disciple of Herodes Atticus, from Thryeatis (Peloponnesus),
Greece, second century CE
Marble
10 3/4 x 6 1/4 x 8 1/4 in.
(27.3 x 16 x 21 cm)
Collection of the Staatliche Museen zu Berlin, Berlin, Germany
Antikensammlung, ID no. SK 1503

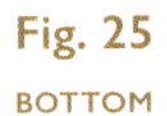

Fig. 25

BOTTOM

Etruscan coins; obverse: head of a Black mahout; reverse: elephant, third century BCE
Bronze
3/4 in. diameter (1.8 cm)
Classical Numismatic Group, Inc.
http://www.cngcoins.com

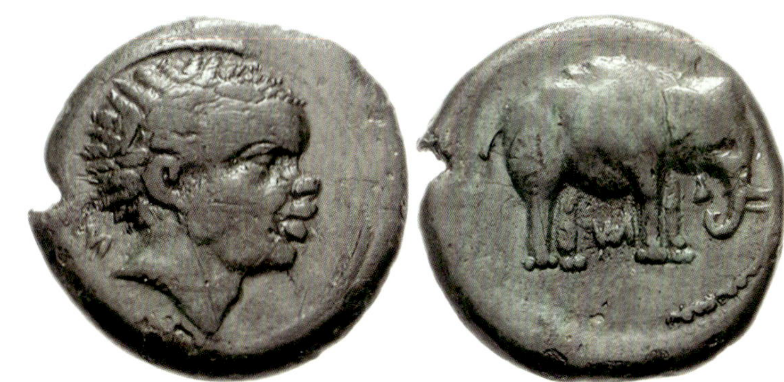

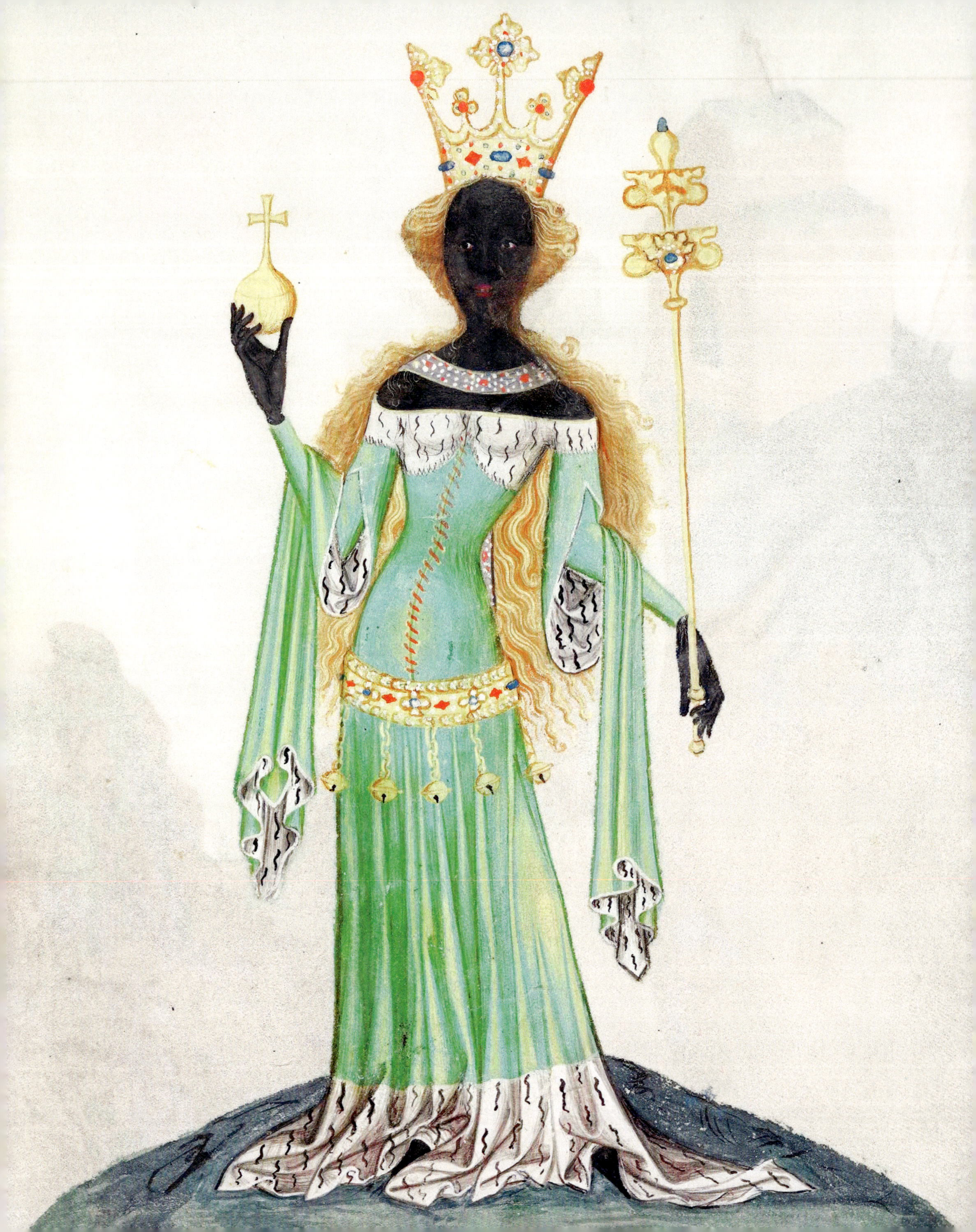

Part Two
The Middle Ages and the Moors

With the fall of Rome in the fourth century CE, Europe was launched into an age of turmoil, marked by one political, military, religious, and health disaster after another. These calamities included savage wars with the Huns from north-central Asia, as well as tribes such as the Ostrogoths, Visigoths, and Vandals from Denmark and Germany, and the Byzantines from Turkey. Far more devastating than war, however, was disease (figs. 26, 27). Between the fifth and seventh centuries, Europe suffered multiple pandemics of typhoid and bubonic plague (the Black Death) that killed an estimated fifty million people (26% of the Western world's population at the time), devastating the continent, drastically reducing its population, and obliterating the advanced infrastructure and cultural progress that the Romans had put into place.

Left

Conrad Kyeser (German, 1366–1405), *Queen of Sheba*, pre-1405
From the illuminated manuscript *Bellifortis, Bohemia*, a manual of military technology
Parchment
Göttingen, Niedersächsische Staats und Universitäsbibliothek, Cod. Philos. 63, folio 122r

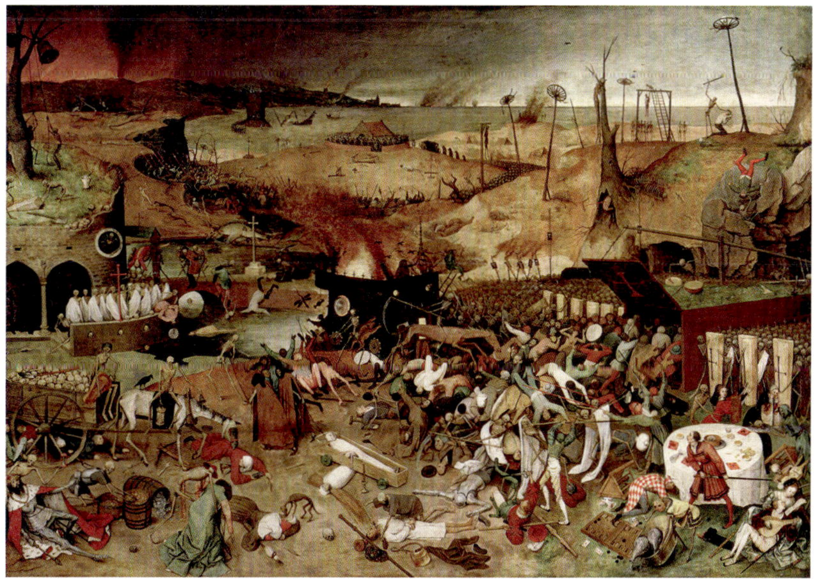

Fig. 26

Pieter Bruegel the Elder (Flemish, ca. 1525–1659), *The Triumph of Death*, ca. 1562
Oil on panel
46 in × 63.8 in (117 x 162 cm)
Collection of the Museo del Prado, Madrid, Spain
Photograph courtesy of Bridgeman Images, Brooklyn, NY

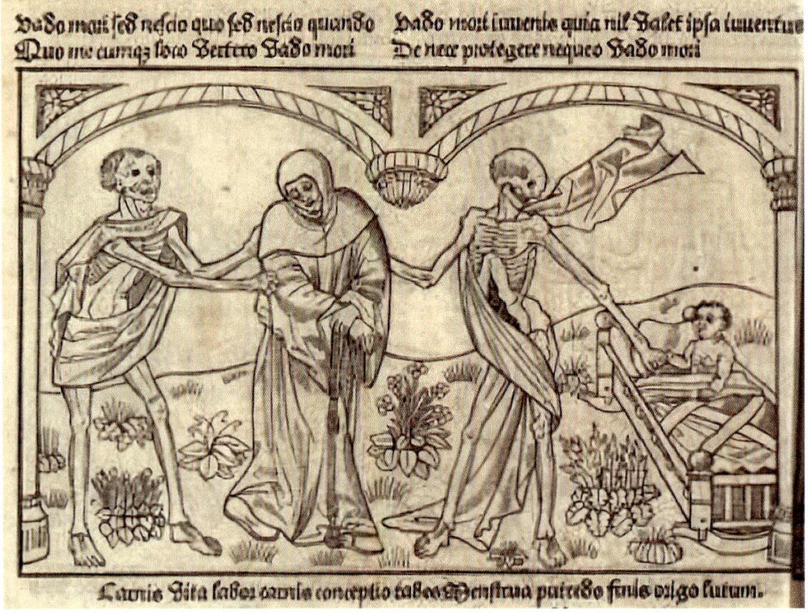

Fig. 27

Guy Marchant (French, 1483–1504), *Death Taking the Beggar and the Child*, from the *Danse Macabre*, manuscript published in Paris, 1485
Woodcut
Private collection

Consequently, much of western Europe was transformed into a depopulated and devastated wasteland. Later, in the eleventh century, Europe experienced a leprosy pandemic followed in the fourteenth century by another round of bubonic plague, which killed no less than 25 million more Europeans (about 50% of the population).[13] During these centuries of the infamous "Dark Ages," Europeans became known to Africans, Arabs, and Byzantines as barbarians, and Europe itself was considered an uncivilized, unlivable place filled with brutish primitives.[14] There was a reprieve during the Gothic era (ca. 1150–1600 CE), which experienced some renewal of prosperity, but not until the advent of the Renaissance was Europe able to fully and permanently replenish its lost population and restore economic and social order.

One other affliction struck Europe during this period—the armies of the newest religion on Earth at the time—Islam. After the death of Muhammad (570–632), his first three successor caliphs, Abu Bakr (633–634), Umar (634–644), and Uthman (644–56),[15] rapidly expanded Muslim rule (fig. 28). Within twenty short years, due to an unstoppable 50,000-man elite cavalry, the Muslims easily outmaneuvered what little resistance they encountered in war- and disease-ravaged Europe (fig. 29).[16] Between 700 and 1400, Muslims overtook Persia, the Byzantine Empire, Italy, North Africa, Spain, Eastern Europe as far north as Hungary, and France (coming to within 100 miles of Paris before being driven back). They ruled this vast empire until Christian Crusaders, beginning in the eleventh century, forced them to retreat to the eastern and southern territories.[17]

Significant about the Muslim invasion of Europe was the Muslim adherence to the Second Commandment: "Thou shalt not make any graven

Fig. 28

The Prophet, 'Ali, Husayn and Hasan in Paradise; 'Uthman, 'Umar and Abu Bakr are in the foreground; miniature from a seventeenth-century manuscript of *Khavarnama*, a poem on the deeds of 'Ali; Punjab, India, 1686 British Library, London, UK

Fig. 29

A map illustrating the rise and expansion of the early Islamic caliphates from the time of the Prophet Muhammad until the ninth century Worldhistory.org (https://www.worldhistory.org/image/14212/islamic-conquests-in-the-7th-9th-centuries/) Created and uploaded by Simeon Netchev

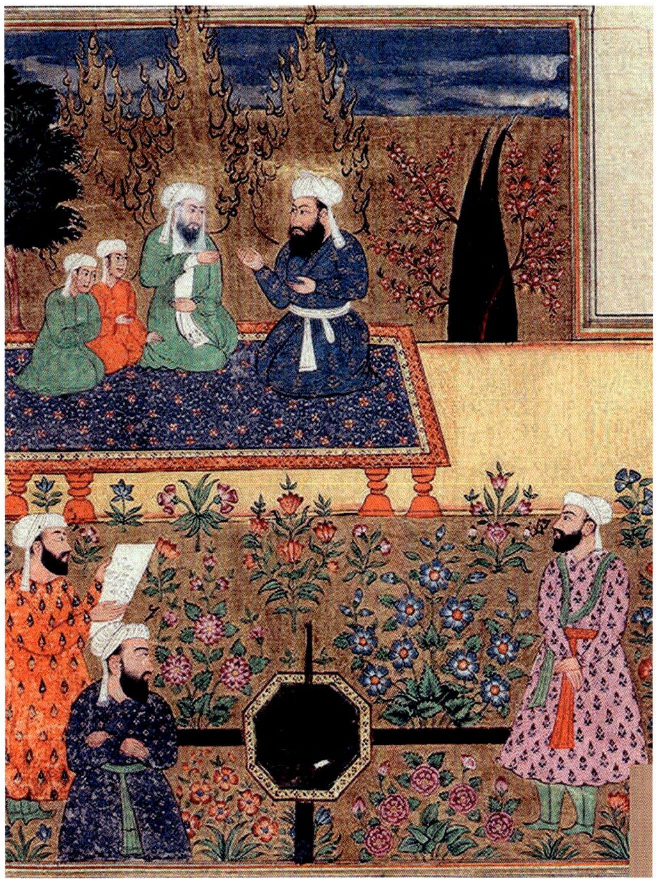

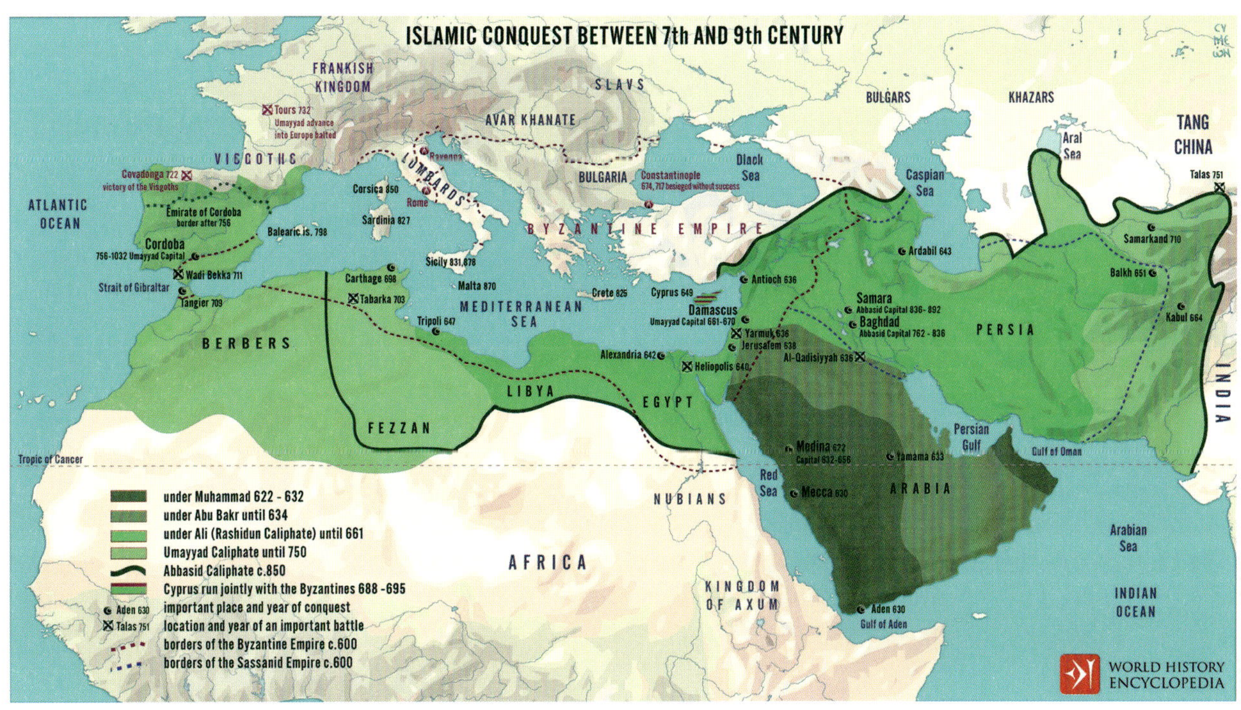

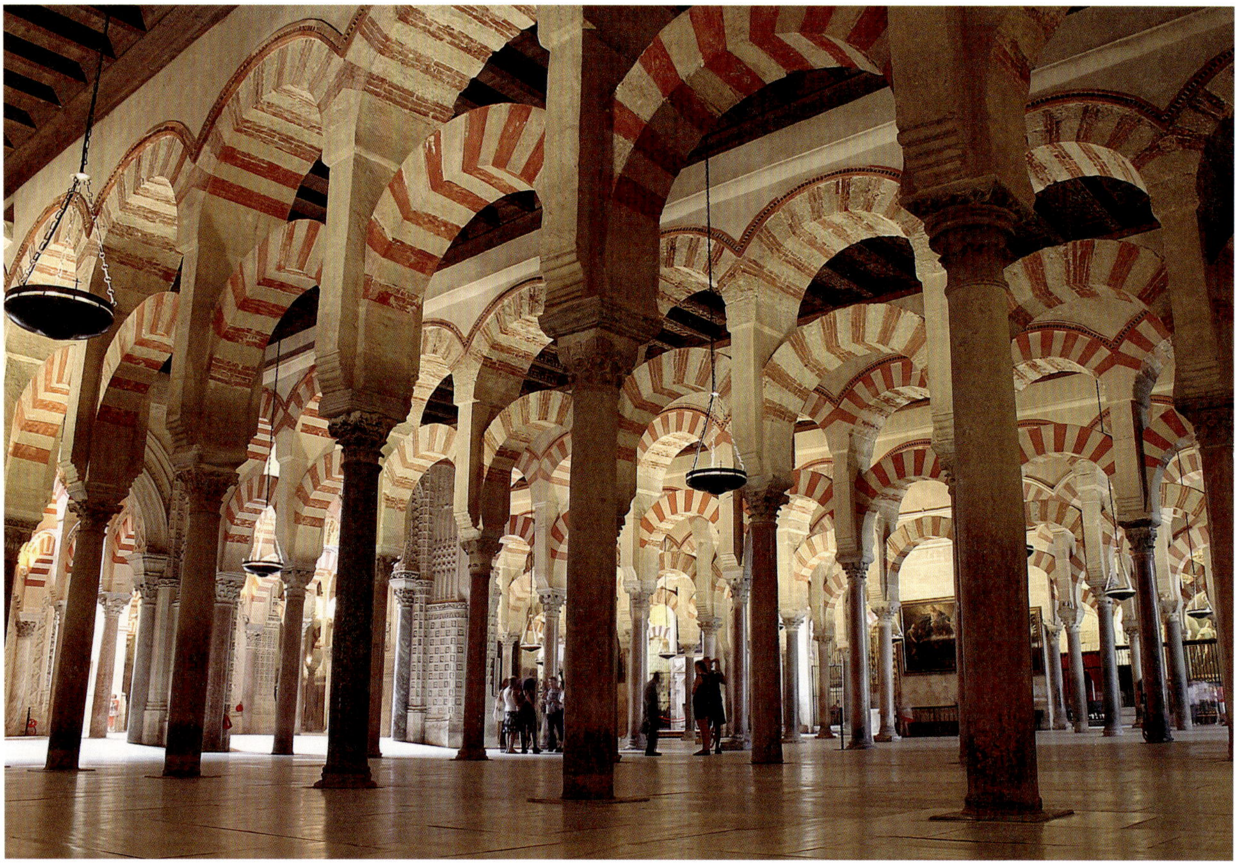

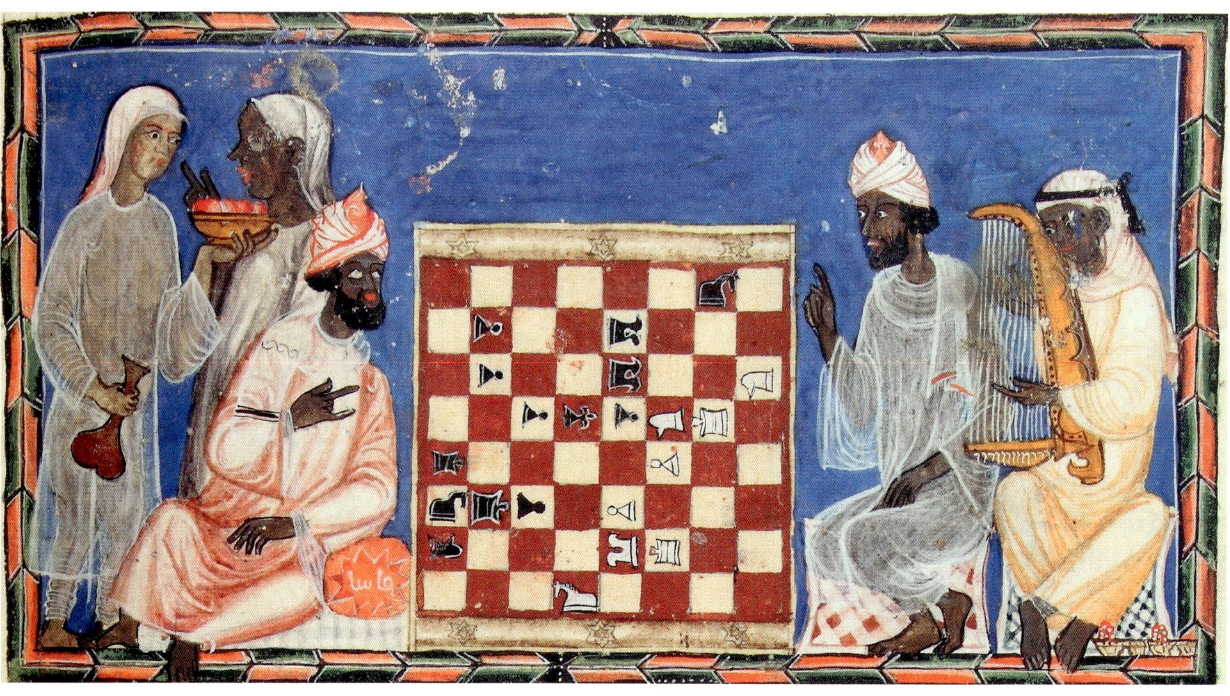

Fig. 30

OPPOSITE, ABOVE

Interior of the Great Mosque at Cordoba, Spain, showing mihrab and bays of two-tiered horseshoe arches, 785
Photograph: Ángel M. Felicísimo at https://www.flickr.com/people/8146925@N08"

Fig. 31

OPPOSITE, BELOW

Alfonso X of Castile the Wise, *Libreo de Juegos o Libro del Ajedrez Dados y Tablas*, 1283, folio 22R of Moros Jugando al Ajedrez Junto a un Musico que Toca el Arpa, 1221–1284
Collection of the Monastery Library, San Lorenzo del Escorial, Madrid, Spain

image or any likeness of anything that is in the Heaven above, that is in the Earth beneath, or that is in the water under the Earth (Exodus 20:4-6)." This ban on artmaking was disregarded by Western Christians after the Iconoclastic Controversies of the eighth century, which authorized religious picture-making despite the Second Commandment. Muslims, however, whose Quran is almost identical to the Bible, rigidly adhered to its edict. The result was that Muslims left behind virtually no visual or artistic records of their presence in Europe, in effect making the erasure of their presence there a simple matter of omitting them from written histories. They did, however, leave behind architectural records, such as the Great Mosque in Cordoba, Spain (fig. 30). It was constructed during the Umayyad Dynasty (661–750) but was converted into a church after the 1236 ousting of Caliph Mohammed ibn Alhamar by Ferdinand III of Castile.[18] Despite the building's reassignment as a Christian church, the distinctive look of its Muslim decoration is undeniable.

Oddly enough, it was the Europeans who recorded the Islamic presence in Europe, creating sculptures and paintings of the Muslims they knew—particularly of Arab and African Muslims or Moors, who made up the rank and file of the Muslim army (fig. 31).[19] Evidence can be seen in a thirteenth-century architectural capital from Troia, Portugal, which depicts the full lips, broad nostril, and coiling hair of an African (fig. 32). During the Muslim jihads, ties between Europe and Christian Africa were severed and, as a result, prejudices began to form in the European psyche. The Moors, with whom

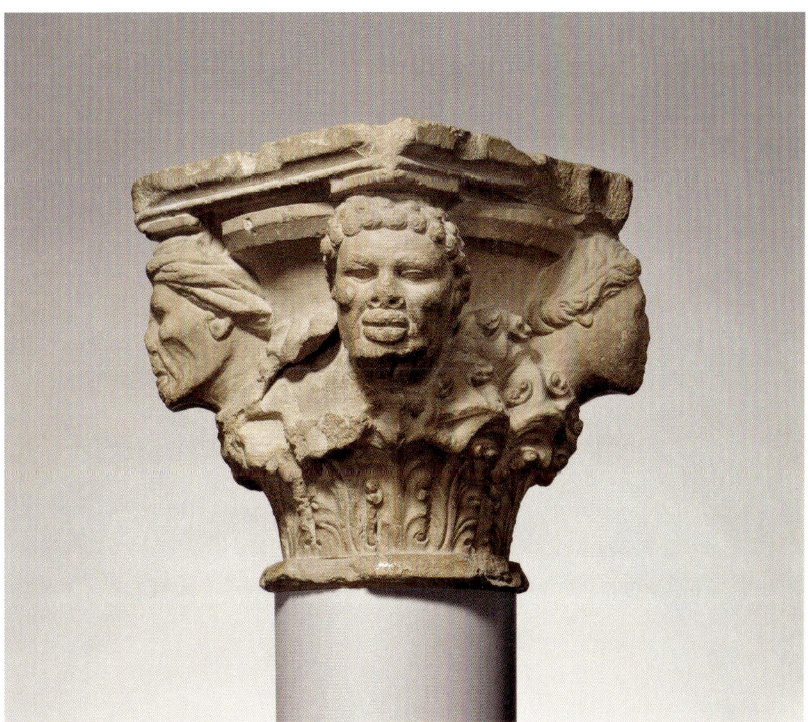

Fig. 32

Capital with Four Heads, ca. 1225–1250
Limestone
14 1/8 x 13 x 13 in. (35.9 x 33 x 33 cm)
The Metropolitan Museum of Art, New York, NY
Gift of James Hazen Hyde, 1955; acc. no: 55.66

Europeans had come into violent contact during the Muslim invasions, began to be cast in a derogatory light, and particularly in Western Europe, "black" became the color of the enemy and the idea of "blackness" was associated with all things non-Christian, including persecution, sin, and evil, as portrayed in a fourteenth century "orphrey" (priestly or knightly robe decoration) from southern England (fig. 33).[20]

In the art of this period, Africans are depicted as biblical executioners or persecutors of Christians. Nevertheless, while these images depict Africans as oppressors, they also portray them as the military and social equals or betters of Europeans, evident in a fourteenth-century illumination of a battle between Muslim and European armies from the epic poem, *The Song of Roland*—the oldest extant work of French literature (fig. 34).[21] Even when viewed as religious adversaries, Blacks were still begrudgingly respected by medieval Europeans. Similarly, a Gothic sculpture from the Rouen Cathedral in France of an African beheading John the Baptist (fig. 35), is a Western depiction of a

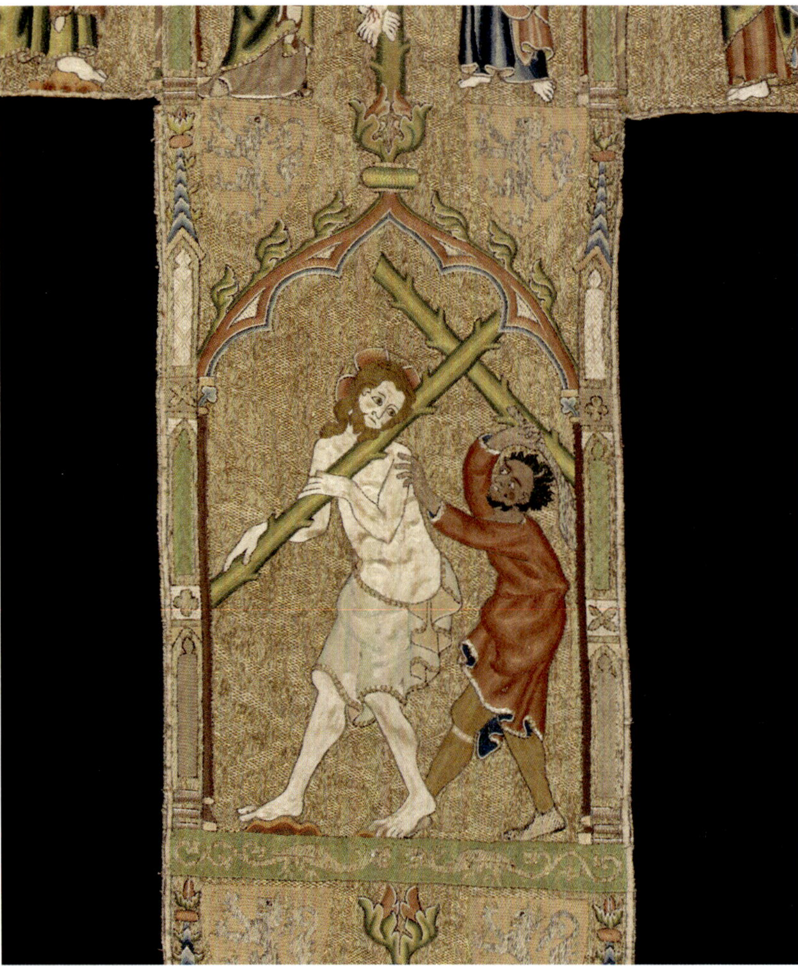

Fig. 33

Christ Carrying the Cross, from the Marnhull orphrey, ca. 1310–1325
Linen with silver, gold, and silk embroidery
Victoria and Albert Museum, London, UK
Photograph courtesy of the Victoria and Albert Museum

Fig. 34

Coronation master of Charles VI, illuminator, Illumination from *The Song of Roland*, 1375-1380, Collection of the Grandes chroniques de France, Bibliothèque nationale de France, Français 2813, folio 121r

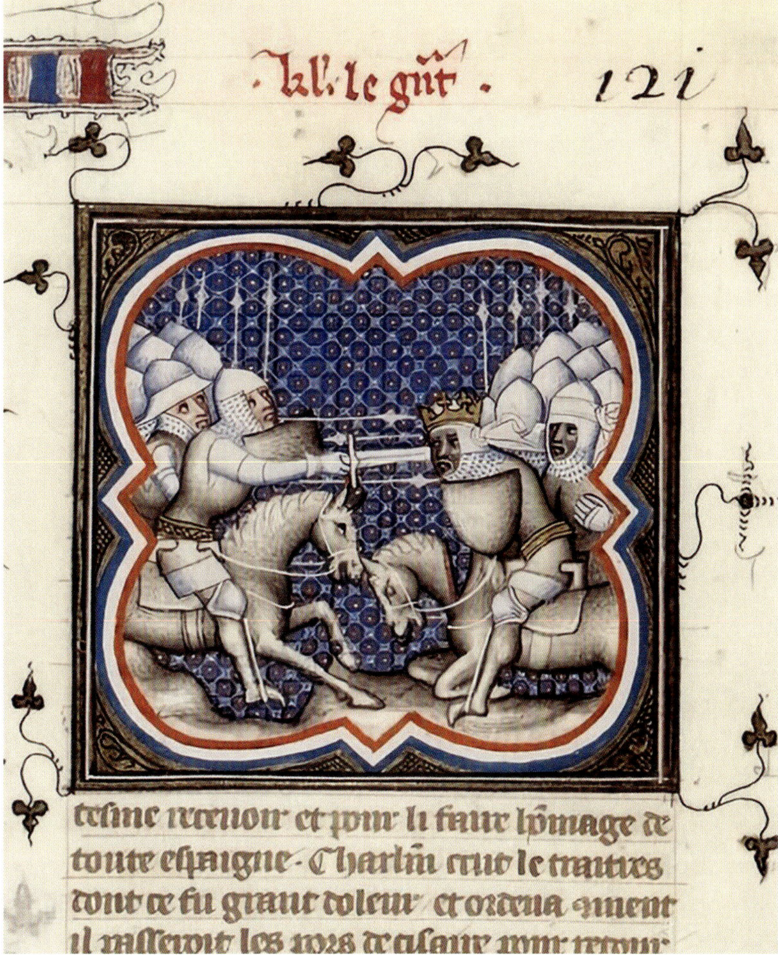

Fig. 35

Notre-Dame Cathedral, Rouen, France, sculpted tympanum of the beheading of St. John the Baptist, ca. 13th century, north portal, west façade
Plaster cast from stone
Musee des Monuments Francais, Paris, France
Photograph courtesy of Bridgeman Images, Brooklyn, NY

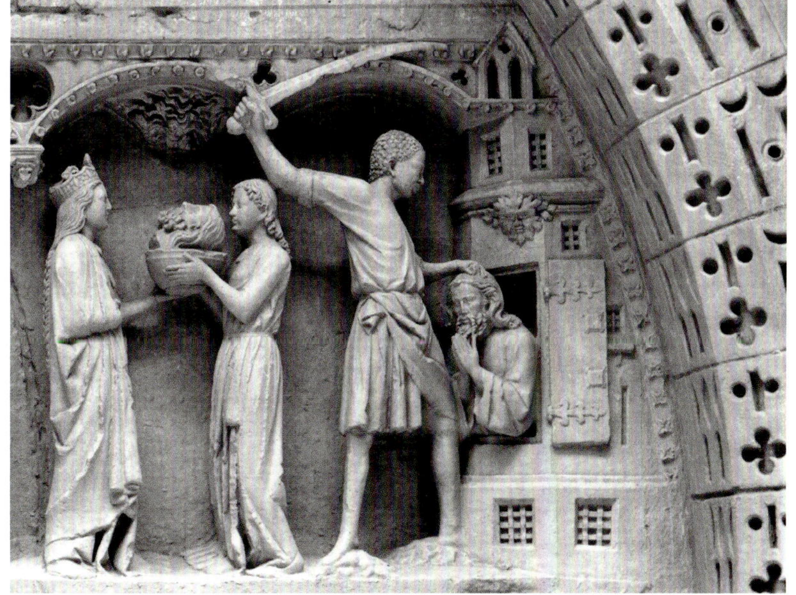

political hierarchy that places Blacks in power while also being an honest and sympathetic portrayal of the Black man wielding the sword. The same can be said of the executioner of John the Baptist in a Gothic Psalter (Book of Psalms) of Louis IX and of an elegant sculpture of a Black executioner from Reims Cathedral, also in France (fig. 36).

During the Middle Ages and the later Renaissance, despite antipathy toward Black Muslims, Europeans felt no such animosity toward Black Christians. On the contrary, they looked to Egyptian and Nubian Christians as their champions who had the potential to save them from the Muslim onslaught.[22] In fact, European art honored Africans as heroes far more often than it maligned them as oppressors.[23] The legend of Prester (minister) John is a good example. It developed in the twelfth century and described a magical and marvelous Ethiopian (Coptic[24]) Christian king who was descended

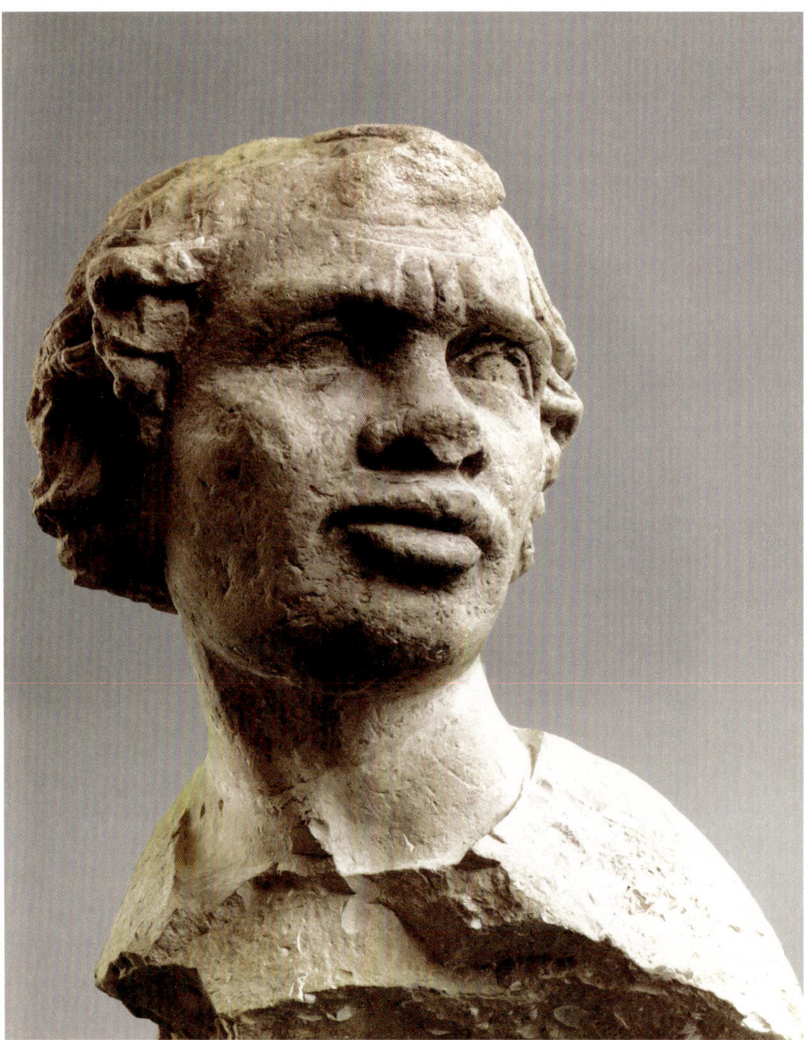

Fig. 36

Executioner's head, fragment from the archivolts of the north door of the west façade of Reims Cathedral, 1247–1255, Reims, France
Collection of the Musée du Tau, Reims, France

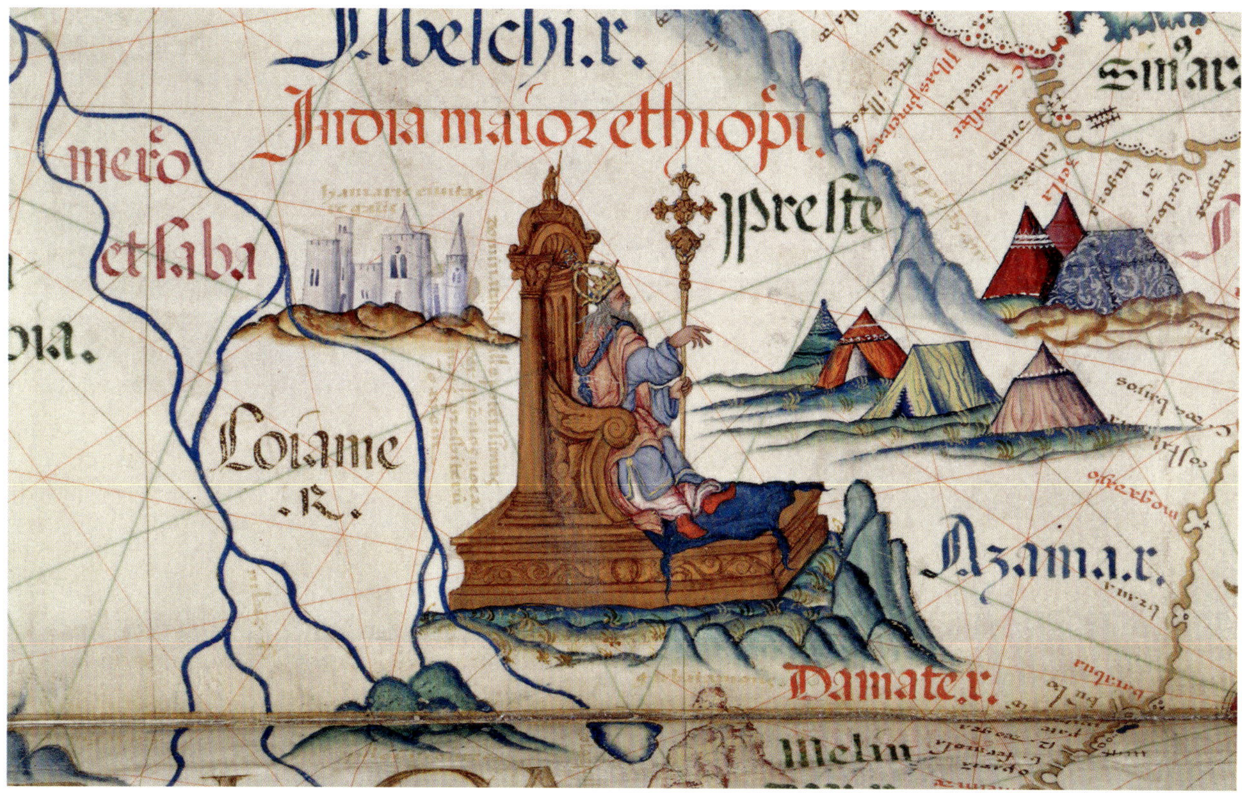

Fig. 37

Detail of Prester John sitting on his throne in Ethiopia; part of a map of East Africa. He was a mythical king, reportedly descended from one of the Three Magi, and said to rule over a Christian kingdom, amidst the pagans, imagined to be Ethiopia, 1558
Pen and ink with watercolor on paper
Collection of the British Library, London, UK.; BL2630707
Photograph courtesy of Bridgeman Images, Brooklyn, NY

from the Magi and hailed as the forthcoming savior of European Christianity. Prester John's legend was based partially in fact because Coptic kings actually did ally themselves with the Spanish Court and an unrealized ninth crusade was planned by European and African Christian allies in the year 1300. As the incarnation of a wealthy African Christian, the legend of Prester John developed into a full-blown European obsession with a mythical Black champion (fig. 37).[25]

From Gothic to Renaissance: St. Maurice and Parzival

A similar fixation among European Christians focused on the Egyptian-born St. Maurice (d. 287), who was not a myth but an actual African commander of Rome's famed Theban Legion from Luxor, Egypt, that fought in Europe during the third century. In 287, when Maurice, a Christian convert, refused an imperial Roman edict requiring him to sacrifice Christian Gauls to the Roman gods of victory, he and his officers were put to death. In fact, the Legion was said to have laid bare their necks willingly for beheading rather than betray God. The martyrs' remains were buried at Aguanum (which is today St. Maurice-en-Valais in Switzerland), where an abbey was established

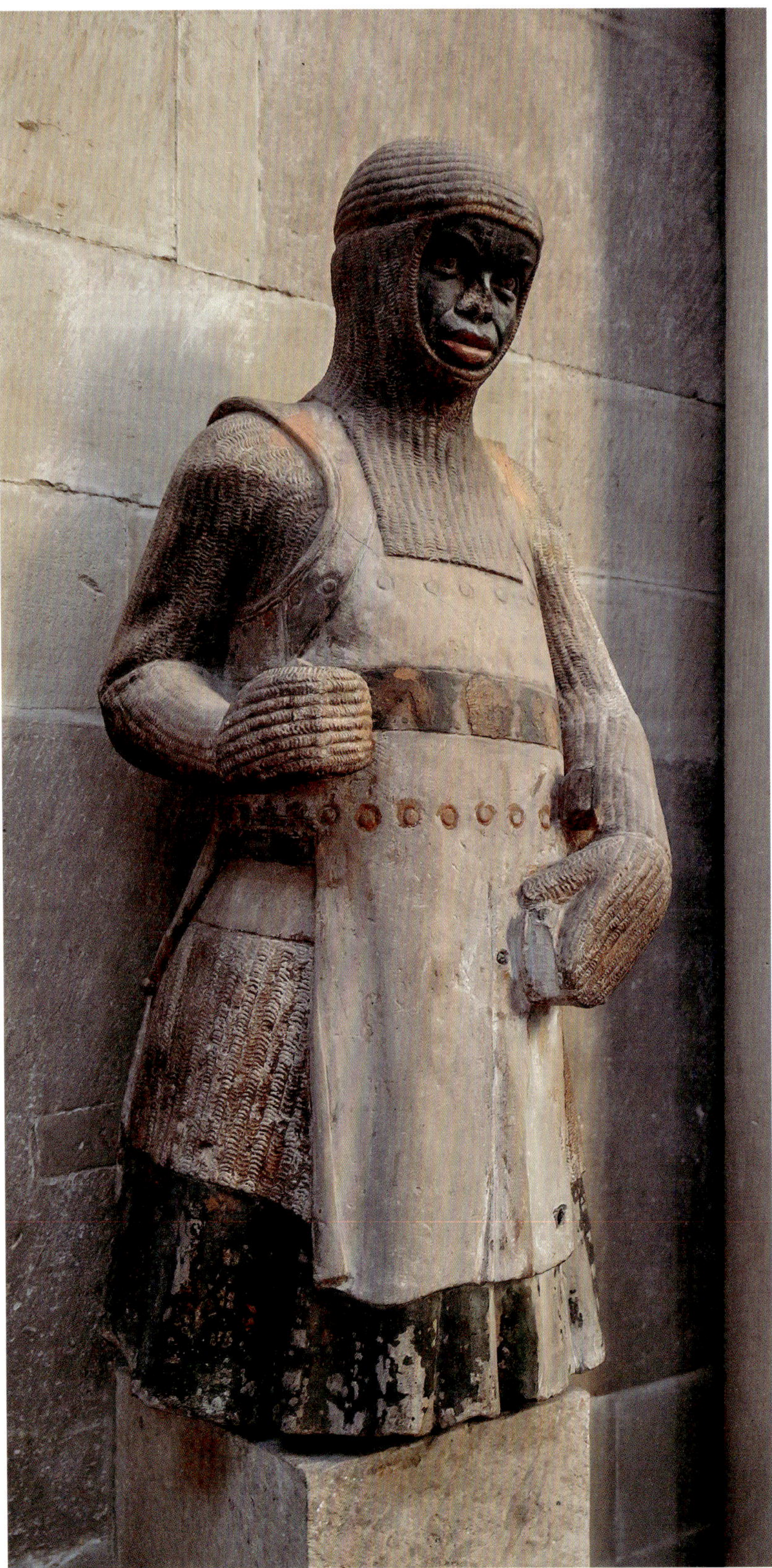

Fig. 38

Statue of Saint Maurice at Magdeburg Cathedral, interior
Magdeburg, Germany
Diego Grandi / Alamy Stock Photo

in their honor in the year 515. The martyrdom of Maurice and his followers was best documented in the fifth century by St. Eucherius, Bishop of Lyon, in his *Passions of the Martyrs of Aguanum*, and modern archaeological evidence suggests that much of Eucherius' account is accurate. So admired was Maurice that he became the center of a knightly order—the Chivalric Order of Saint Maurice founded in 1434 by the French Duke of Savoy—and he was the patron saint of German soldiers and celebrated among the Saxon nobility. In fact, in the tenth century, the German Emperor Otto I adopted Maurice as his royal patron and as the patron of the Holy Roman Empire. From the tenth to the fifteenth centuries, Maurice's image as a Black knight appeared often in architectural reliefs, paintings, and illuminated manuscripts. Overemphasizing the saint's African features, the German sculptor of a carving that adorned the Magdeburg Cathedral in Germany dressed the saint in knightly attire, so as to associate him with the contemporaneous age (fig. 38).

In 1504, the famed German Renaissance artist, Matthais Grünewald, painted a work depicting Saints Maurice and Erasmus (fig. 39). The artist modernized the Roman saints by placing them in the roles of Erasmus as

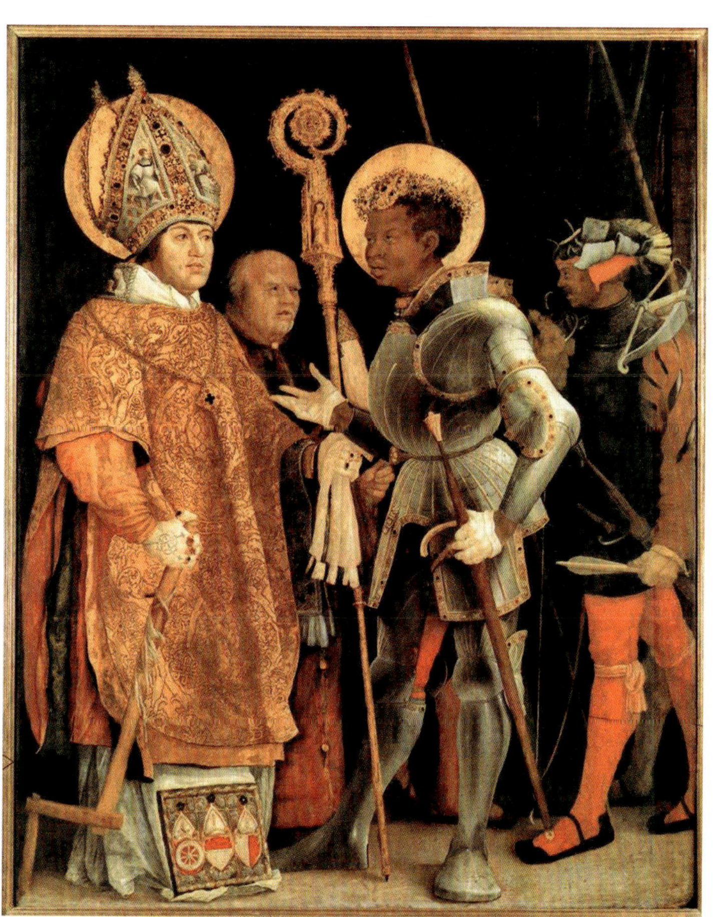

Fig. 39

Matthias Grünewald (German, 1470–1528), *Meeting of St. Maurice and St. Erasmus*, 1520–1524
Oil on panel
89 x 70 1/16 in. (226 x 176 cm)
Alte Pinakothek, Munich, Germany

a European Pope soliciting aid for the Crusades from a wealthy African Christian—Maurice—who sports gold and silver armor, white gloves, a halo, and a gold filigree crown. Saints Maurice and Erasmus are well-paired by Grünewald because both lived and died as martyrs in the fourth century and both were military men. Maurice is the patron of soldiers and Erasmus of sailors. So revered were the two that German leaders of the age self-identified with them. For example, in the Grünewald painting, St. Erasmus bears the features of Albrecht von Brandenburg, Archbishop of Magdeburg, who was a papal cardinal. Albrecht's predecessor as Archbishop of Magdeburg, Ernest, is portrayed as Maurice in Peter Vischer's 1495 *Funerary Monument of Archbishop Ernest of Saxony* as Saint Maurice, also from the Magdeburg Cathedral (fig. 40). The likeness for Archbishop Ernest was borrowed from the relief of St. Maurice on the crown of the reclining figure of Ernest from the same monument. Maurice was revered as one of the patron saints of Halle, where Albrecht von Brandenburg resided and founded a church to house more than 8,000 holy relics, many associated with Maurice. Although Albrecht's vast collection of relics no longer exists, it was carefully documented in an illuminated relic book—the famed *Hallesches Heiltumsbuch (Halle Relic Book)*.[26]

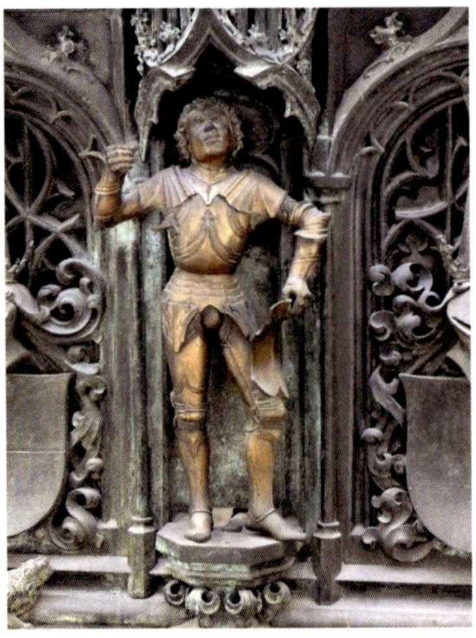

Fig. 40

Peter Vischer, *Funerary Monument of Archbishop Ernest of Saxony,* Magdeburg Cathedral, Germany, 1495
Detail of Ernest as St. Maurice

The Reformation, launched in 1517 with Martin Luther's *95 Theses*, harshly critiqued the church for its emphasis on wealth and power, and for its sale of "indulgences" (quicker access to heaven for those who made donations to the Church to buy relics). Martin Luther's protest campaign ultimately resulted in a loss of interest in images of a wealthy Maurice after 1540. In fact, Martin Luther's *Theses* were directly prompted by Albrecht von Brandenburg's abuse of the indulgences practice to enhance his status and political power while also purchasing relics. As late as 1525, however, a depiction of Maurice was painted by Lucas Cranach the Elder, showing the saint wearing solid silver and gold armor (fig. 41). It documents the sumptuous and princely nature attributed to the saint by Church officials. From the Halle Domkirsch in Germany, this painting was likely the left panel of an altarpiece created for Albrecht's collection. The painting portrays Maurice holding the hilt of a gilded sword, wearing a modish red velvet hat trimmed with ostrich feathers, and gripping the standard of the German royal state (on the left of which is visible a portion of the wings of the Brandenburg eagle).

The Cranach painting is a visual record of a no-longer-extant, life-size silver gilt sculpture of Maurice that was one of the relics owned by Albrecht and recorded in his relic book. The statue was displayed as part of a grand theatrical *mise-en-scène* at his church in Halle and annually paraded in an elaborate procession. This spectacular suit of armor made the Halle church one of Europe's most significant pilgrimage sites. Indeed, untold journeys were made by the faithful throughout Saxony to honor Maurice, the most popular German saint of the age. The original statue was ultimately destroyed when, in 1541, thanks to Martin Luther's protests against the Catholic Church, the

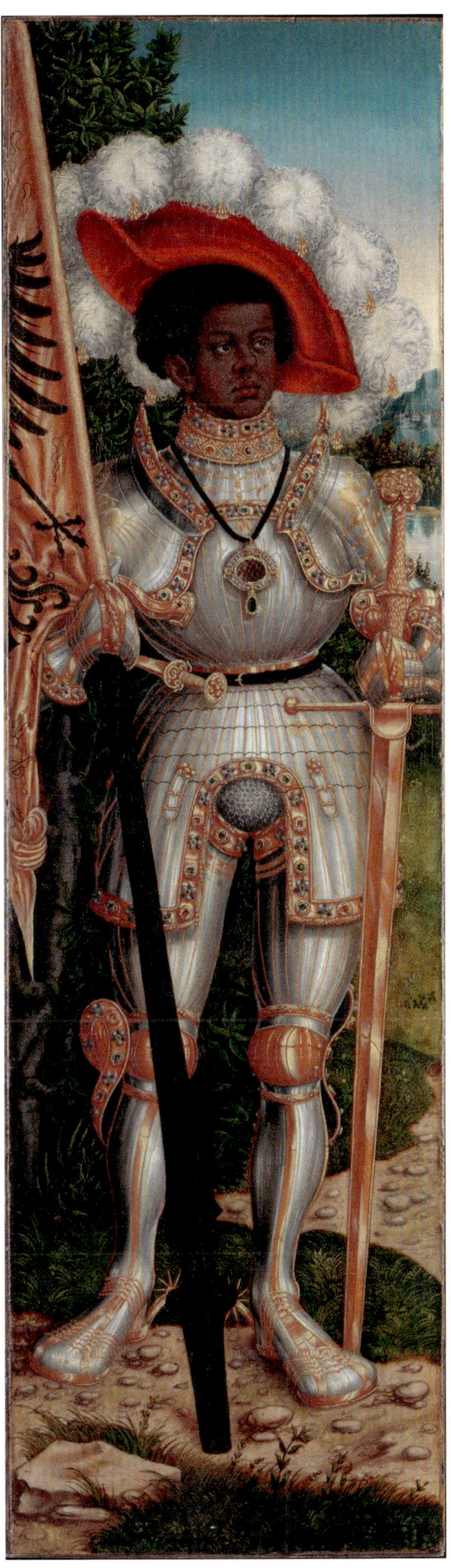

Fig. 41

Lucas Cranach, the Elder (German, 1472–1553), and workshop, *St. Maurice*, 1525
Oil on linden board
54 x 15½ in. (137.2 x 39.4 cm), altarpiece left wing of the Halle Marketkirsch, Germany, commissioned by Cardinal Albrecht de Brandenburg
The Metropolitan Museum of Art, New York, NY
Bequest of Eva F. Kollsman, 2005; acc. no: 2006.469

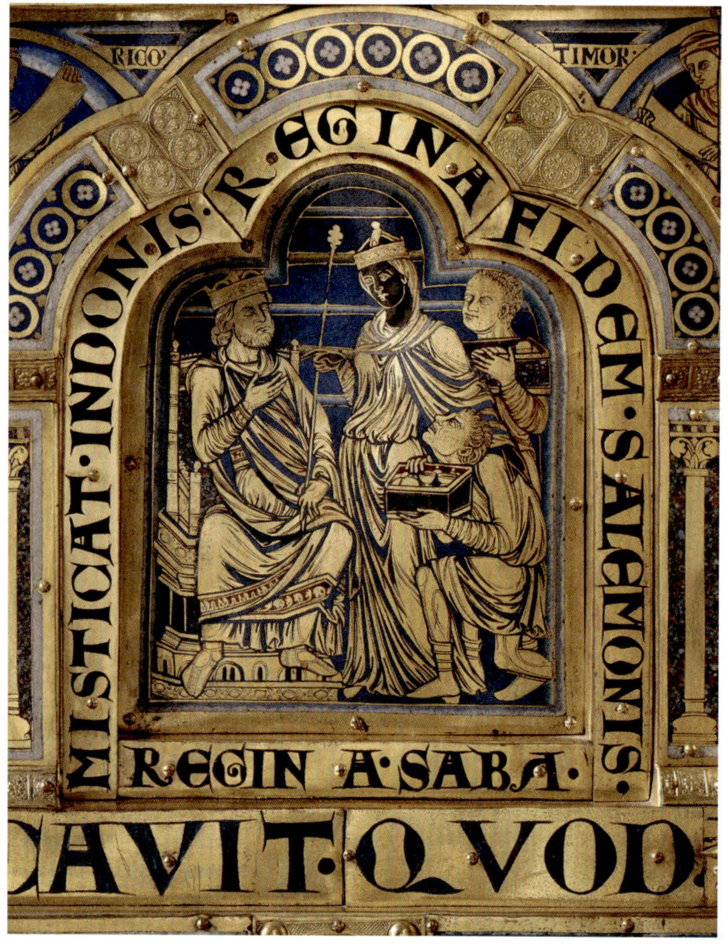

Fig. 42

Nicolas of Verdun (French, ca. 1130–1205),
Verdun Altar, ca.1181
Gold and enamel, 51 panels in
3 horizontal tiers
Detail representing the Queen of Sheba
bringing gifts to King Solomon
The Klosterneuburg Monastery,
Klosterneuburg, Austria
Photograph courtesy of Bridgeman Images,
Brooklyn, NY

Fig. 43

BELOW

Madonna of Częstochowa,
12th century?
Tempera on primed canvas board
$53\frac{15}{16} \times 38\frac{3}{16}$ in. (137 × 97 cm)
Jasna Gora Monastery,
Częstochowa, Poland
Photograph courtesy of Wikimedia
Commons

Fig. 44

OPPOSITE

The Virgin of Montserrat (La Moreneta),
pre-718?
Gilded wood
38 in. high (96.5 cm)
Santa Maria de Montserrat Abbey,
Catalonia, Spain
Photograph courtesy of
Wikimedia Commons

city of Halle itself converted to Protestantism. Albrecht had the statue melted down to pay his debts and was compelled to retreat to northwest Bavaria.

St. Maurice and Prester John were joined by a number of other Blacks who, by the 1400s, had ushered in the so-called "African Century" in Europe.[27] They included the biblical Queen of Sheba (who was first depicted as Black in late-twelfth-century German art). Her dark complexion alludes to the queen's Ethiopian or Middle Eastern birth; to the fact that, in Coptic literature, she and Solomon bore an Ethiopian son; and to the words from the biblical Song of Solomon, "I am black and comely, oh ye daughters of Jerusalem" (pp. 17, 36; fig. 42). Similarly, a proliferation of Black Madonnas was created beginning in the Byzantine era and continuing through the Renaissance (figs. 43, 44), as well as images of the African King Balthazar, one of the three Magi, who appears in Gothic and Renaissance paintings of the Adoration. In a 1494 Renaissance painting by Hieronymus Bosch, the Black King is represented much like Saint Maurice, as a wealthy nobleman wearing gold jewelry and elaborately embroidered and pleated white robes to suggest his wealth, nobility,

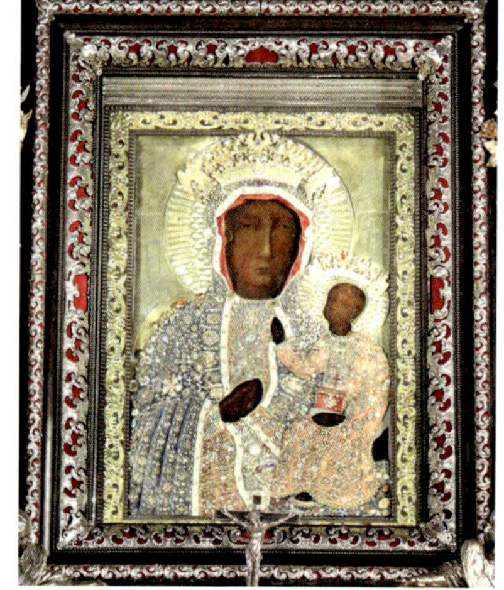

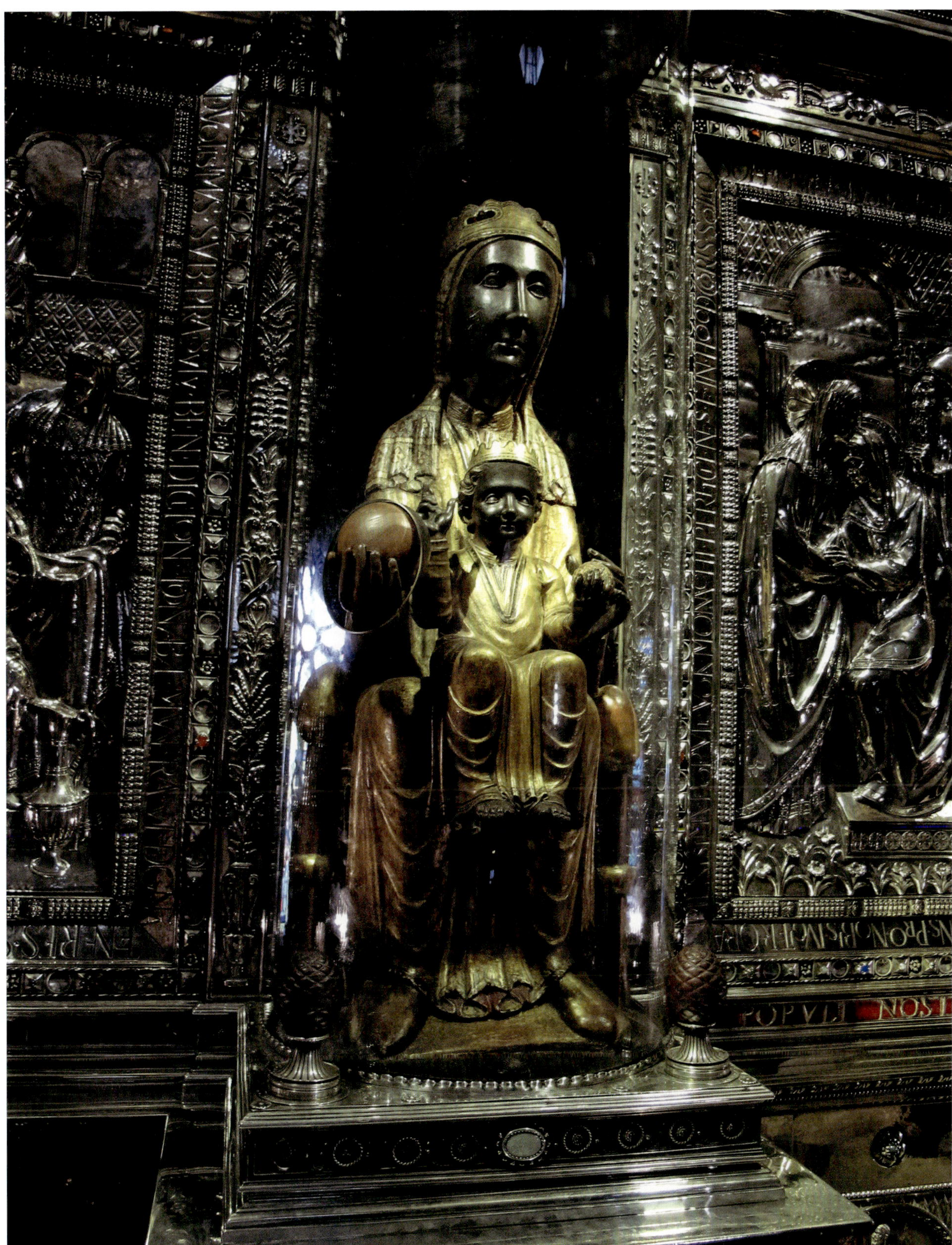
POPVLI

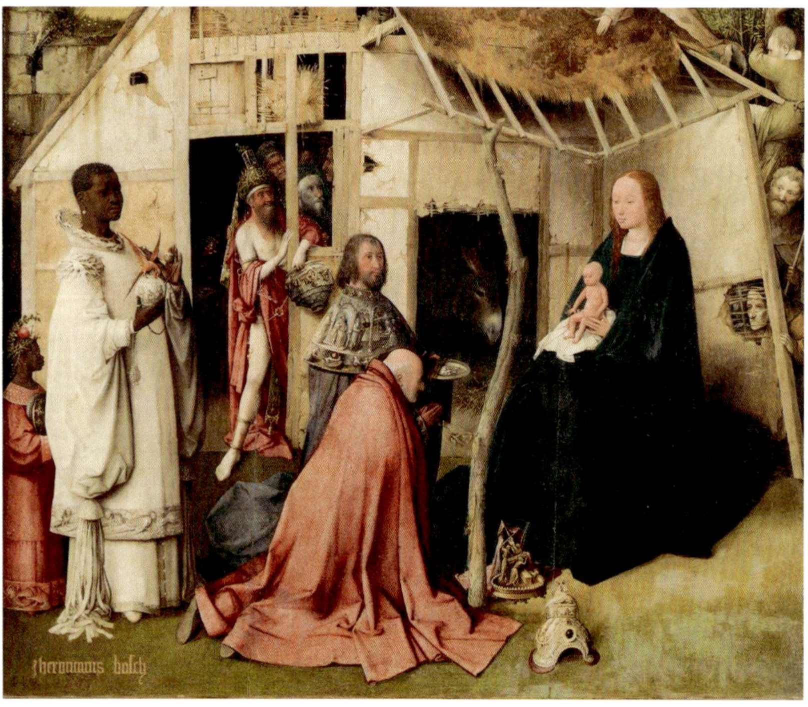

Fig. 45

Hieronymus Bosch (Dutch, ca. 1450–1516), *The Adoration of the Magi*, ca. 1494, detail of central panel of triptych
Oil on oak panel
58 1/16 × 66 3/8 in. (147.4 × 168.6 cm)
Museo del Prado, Madrid, Spain

and purity. He also carries an ornate silver and gold censer, filled with frankincense for the Christ child. An exotic bird perches on top of the censer, reinforcing the Black king's access to rare things—not unlike the European nobles who identified with him (fig. 45).

In its admiration for wealthy and saintly Africans, medieval Europe also produced an epic work of literature entitled *Perceval* (or *Parzival* in German)—an Arthurian romance about the Holy Grail. The epic was considered one of the greatest works of medieval literature second only to Dante's *Divine Comedy*. Written between 1181 and 1200 by Chrétien de Troyes and Wolfram von Eschenbach—the authors of the two most popular versions—this epic poem consists of nearly 25,000 rhymed couplets and was produced in more than five versions in forty years. It was so widely read that seventeen complete handwritten copies and fifty fragments of the original manuscript still exist today—making it a rare primary-source written document that can be studied in its original form (figs. 46, 47).

The German version of this tale features two heroes, Parzival and his Moorish half-brother, Feirefiz, whose persona, not surprisingly, resembled that of Saint Maurice. Feirefiz was a Black prince, a Christian convert, and one of King Arthur's knights. He was the son of a queen named Balacane (famed for her moral purity and midnight-black skin), and of the French knight Gahmuret, who had married Belacane after saving her storied kingdom of Zazamanc from foreign invaders. Being a quintessential knight, however, he quickly tired of married life and, preferring combat to domesticity, deserted Belacane, who was pregnant with their son Feirefiz. Gahmuret went on to fight other battles, save other damsels in distress, and live the life of a roving knight, which included marrying a second queen (of Wales) and fathering a son with her named Parzival.

When both of Gahmuret's sons reached adulthood, they accidentally met in battle—at first not realizing that they were brothers. When Parzival's sword broke during a joust, the fair-minded Moorish Prince Feirefiz proved his gallantry by allowing his opponent to rest before re-arming himself.

Fig. 46

BELOW

Chrétien de Troyes (French, ca. 1130–1190), *Perceval*, ca. 1182–1190 Cover page of thirteenth-century manuscript, produced in France

Fig. 47

RIGHT

Wolfram von Eschenbach (German, 1170–1220), section title page from the *Codex Manesse*, ca. 1300–1340 The *Codex Manesse*, also known as the *Great Heidelberg Book of Songs*, was created in Zürich and is the most comprehensive collection of ballads and epigrammatic poetry in the Middle High German language; it consists of 426 parchments leaves, each 14 × 9 13/16 in. (35.5 x 25 cm), double-sided Universitätsbibliothek Heidelberg, Cod. Pal. germ. 848, fol. 149v: Herr Wolfram von Eschenbach, 1305–1315, Große Heidelberger Liederhandschrift

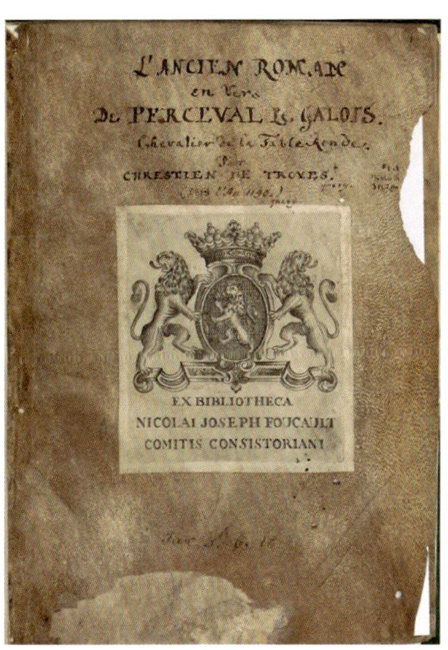

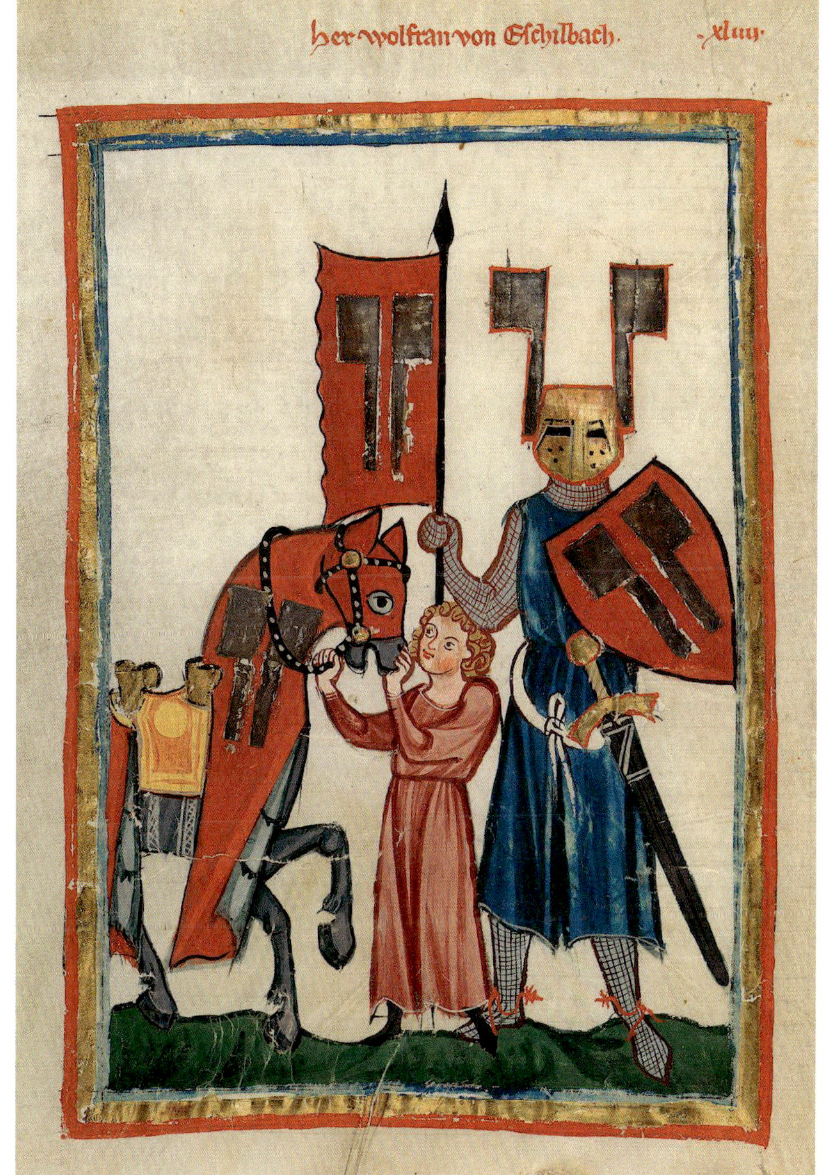

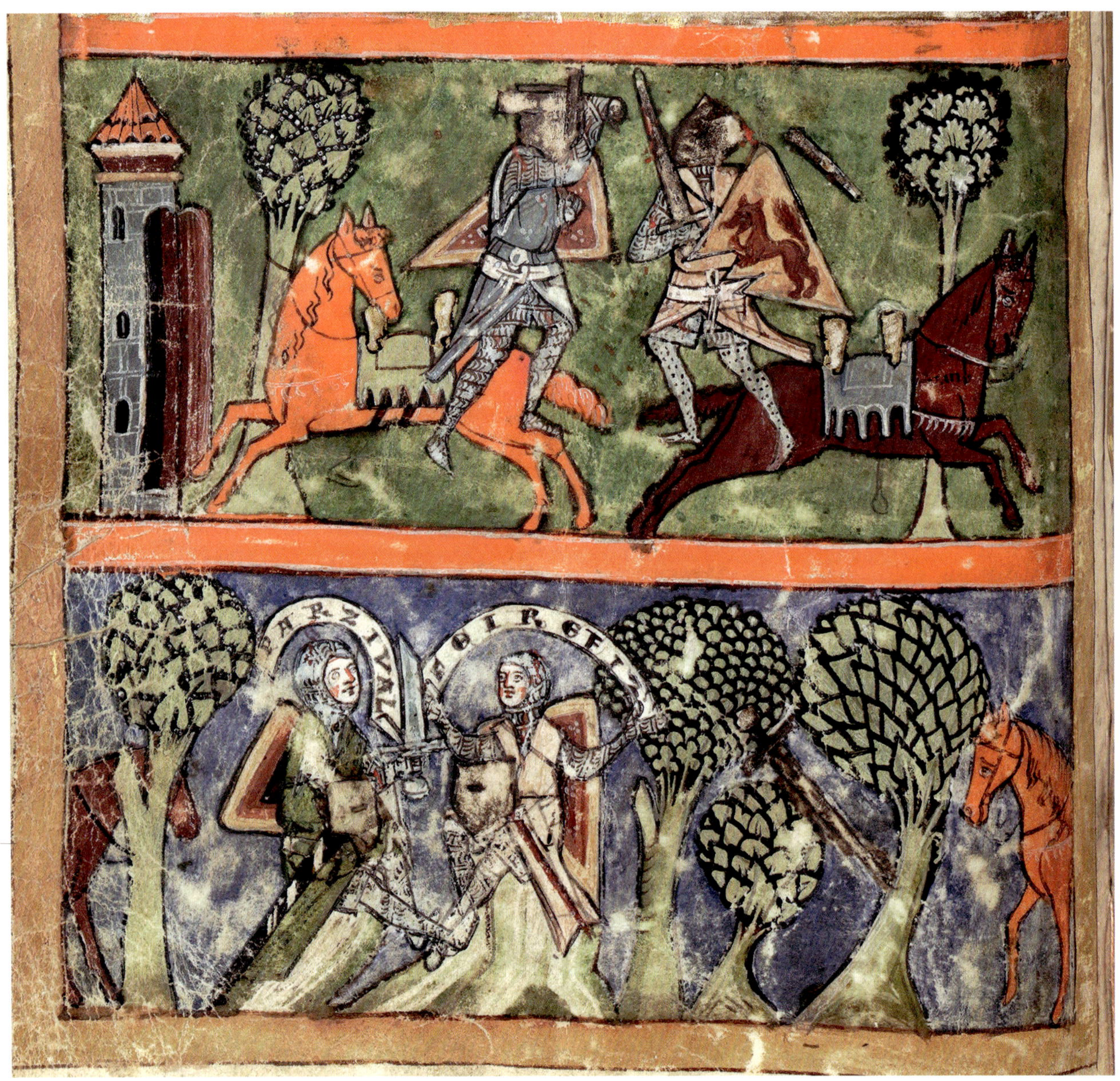

While resting, the two men began to talk and discovered that they had the same father (fig. 48). From then on, they were inseparable. Feirefiz and Parzival joined King Arthur's knights and successfully sought out the Holy Grail. The epic ends by stating that the two princes—one Black and one White—were equal in greatness: "Rich then, beyond all reckoning, I swear were two men here on Earth, Parzival his lordship here; and Feirefiz his only peer" (figs. 49a, 49b).[28]

Fig. 48

Wolfram von Eschenbach (German, 1170–1220), *Parzival with his half-brother, the Infidel Feirefiz*, from a 1240 illuminated manuscript
11 13/16 x 8 1/4 in. (30 x 21 cm)
Folio 49v, State Library, Munich, Germany

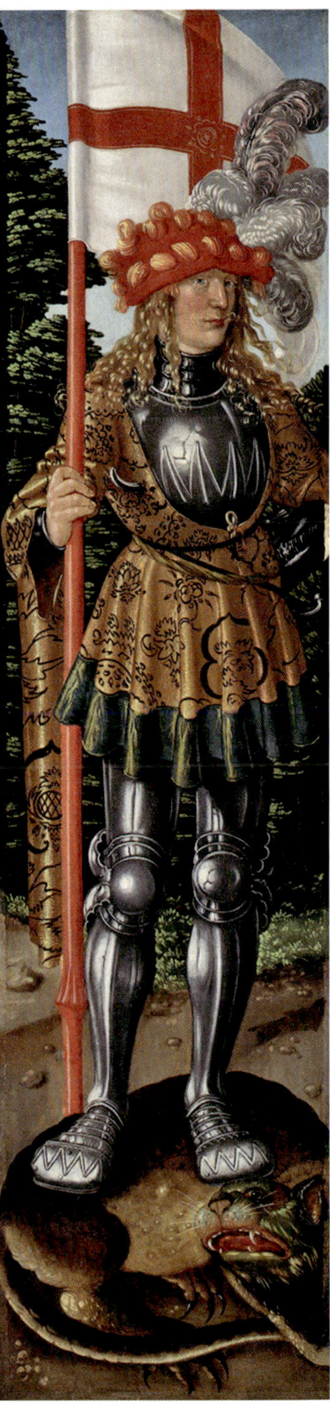

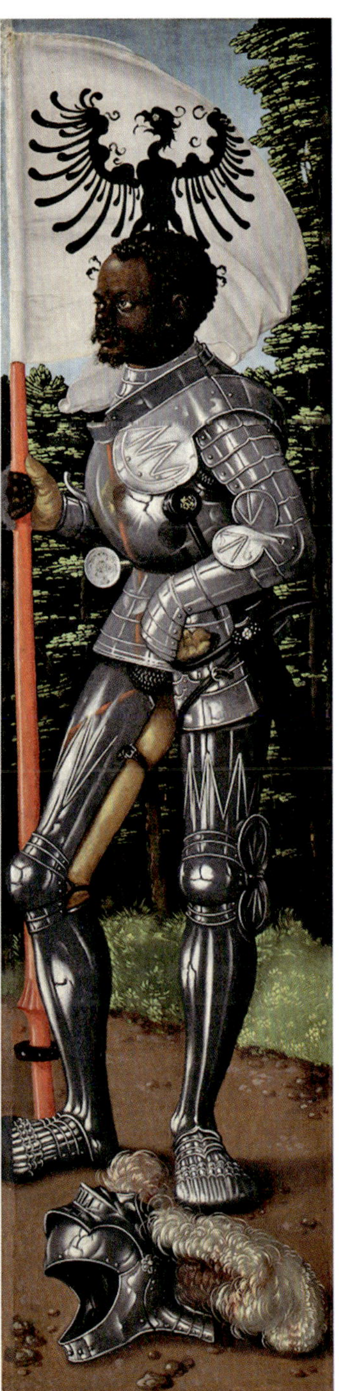

Figs. 49a and b

Hans Baldung Grien (German, 1485–1545), *Saints George and Maurice* (exemplifying Parzival and Feirefiz), 1507
Side panels from the exterior of the *Three Kings* altarpiece
Llinden panel
47 1/16 x 11 in. (121 x 28 cm)
Staatliche Museen, Berlin, Germany

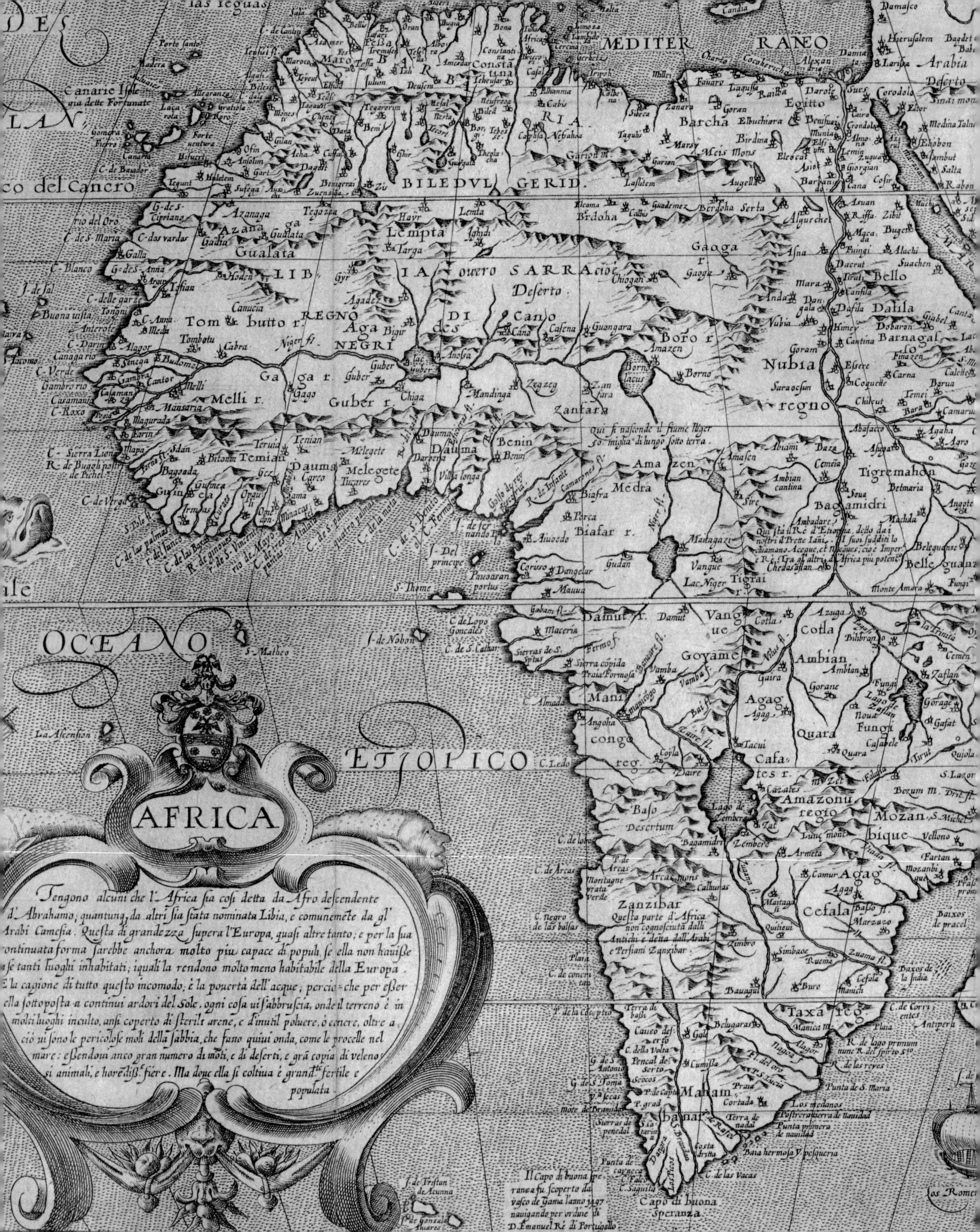

AFRICA
Tengono alcuni che l'Africa sia così detta da Afro descendente
d'Abrahamo; quantunq, da altri sia stata nominata Libia, e comunemēte da gl'
Arabi Camesia. Questa di grandezza supera l'Europa, quasi altre tanto; e per la sua
continuata forma sarebbe anchora molto piu capace di populi, se ella non hauiße
se tanti luoghi inhabitati; iquali la rendono molto meno habitabile della Europa.
E la cagione di tutto questo incomodo; è la pouertà dell'acque; percio=che per eßer
ella sottoposta a continui ardori del Sole, ogni cosa ui s'abbruscia, onde il terreno è in
molti luoghi inculto, ansi coperto di sterili arene, e d'inutil poluere, ò cenere, oltre a
ciò ui sono le pericolose moli della sabbia, che fano quiui onda, come le procelle nel
mare: eßendoui anco gran numero di mōti, e di deserti, e grā copia di veleno-
si animali, e horēdiß. fiere. Ma doue ella si coltiua è grand.te fertile e
populata.
Il Capo di buona spe-
ranza fu scoperto da
vasco de Gama l'anno 1497
nauigando per ordine di
D. Emanuel Rè di Portugallo
Capo di buona
Speranza
OCEANO
ETIOPICO
MEDITER RANEO
BILEDVL GERID.
LIB IA ouero SARRA
REGNO DI
NEGRI
Tombutto r.
Gaga r.
Melli r.
Guber r.
Boro r.
Nubia
regno
Bagamidri
Tigremahon
Amazonu
regio
Mozanbique
Zanzibar
Cefala
Taxa reg.
Manicongo
Goyame
Cafates r.
Barnagal
Dafila
Bello
Gaoga
Egitto
Barcha
Gualata
Lempta
Zanfara
Benin
Melegete
Temian
Medra
Biafar r.
Amazen
Canarie Isole
gia dette Fortunate
co del Cancro

Part Three

European Ascendancy: From Slavs to Slaves

Despite the existence of ample historic artifacts that portrayed Africans as conquerors and as esteemed allies, heroes, and citizens of Europe, few of their images are known to us today. The people who actually shouldered the burden of medieval ethnic bigotry for centuries were Europeans, not Africans, specifically Eastern Europeans or Slavs, from whence the word "slave" derives (fig. 50). Between the fall of Rome and the Renaissance, one of Europe's main marketable exports was slaves, captured from the Slavic nations and sold farther east. Muslims and Byzantines referred to these European slaves as "savages." After the fifteenth century, however, the term "savage" was transferred first to Native Americans in the New World and then, by the eighteenth century, to Blacks, thanks to the African slave trade, which by then was booming in an effort to supply labor to support the rapid colonization of the Americas by Europe.[29] The distance across the Atlantic from West Africa to the Americas was, at its shortest point, less than 2,000 miles. Alternatively, the shortest distance from the Slavic states of Central and Eastern Europe to the Americas was twice that, and involved a lengthy land journey in addition to the ocean crossing. Needless to say, in terms of a slave population, it was far more efficient, both economically and logistically, to draw on the peoples of West Africa rather than Central and Eastern Europe. Thus began the transatlantic slave trade.

Left

Detail of fig. 53, *Map of Africa*, p. 59

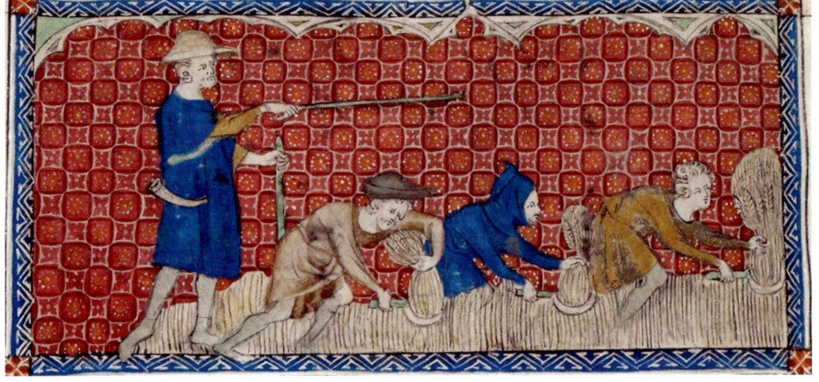

Fig. 50

Queen Mary Master, *Reeve (Overseer) and Serfs Harvesting Wheat with Reaping-hooks*, ca. 1310–1320
From August calendar page of the Queen Mary's Psalter, Westminster, London, or East Anglia
The British Library, London, UK
Ms Royal 2 B.VII , folio 78v

Despite abundant evidence of Africa's political, religious, and social achievements, by the eighteenth and nineteenth centuries, to counteract nascent abolitionist sentiment, European authors, historians, and scientists began to refer to Africa as a land without a history (fig. 51). Renaissance admiration for Africa's numerous and elaborate court systems and its far-reaching network of developed cities evaporated by the eighteenth century (fig. 52). Motivated by a sense of racial and national superiority, colonial explorers provided Europe with distorted accounts of Africa as an uncharted, near-impenetrable jungle when, in reality, a well-traveled system of trade routes had spanned the continent for centuries (fig. 53). European explorers did not, in fact, traverse uncharted lands, but merely asked for directions from Africans who served as their guides and translators.[30] This becomes obvious in an 1872 sketch made of the famed journalist and ex-British soldier Sir Henry Morton Stanley at his hotel in Tanzania after finding the Scottish missionary and "lost" explorer Dr. David Livingstone, not in the jungle, but at the Arab settlement of Ujiji on the eastern shore of Lake Tanganyika (fig. 54).

Wildly popular illustrated accounts of the perilous "Dark Continent" were greatly exaggerated by authors who, in many cases, had never set foot in Africa (fig. 55).[31] Even those like Stanley, who had visited Africa, managed

Fig. 51

BOTTOM, LEFT

J. Chapman, volume 2 frontispiece engraving from Ebenezer Sibly, *An Universal System of Natural History: Including the Natural History of Man, the Orang-Outang and the Whole Tribe of the Simia*, 1795
Coloured engraving with watercolor
3 1/2 × 4 7/8 in. (9 × 12.3 cm)
After Johann-Eberhard Ihle, platemark I; Wellcome Collection
Source: Wellcome Collection

Fig. 52

BOTTOM, RIGHT

James William Buell (American, 1849–1920), *A Buffalo Turns Hunter*, engraving from page 142 of the book *Heroes of the Dark Continent: A Complete History of All the Great Explorations and Discoveries in Africa from the Earliest Ages to the Present Time*
Philadelphia, PA, and St. Louis, MO: Historical Publishing Company, 1879

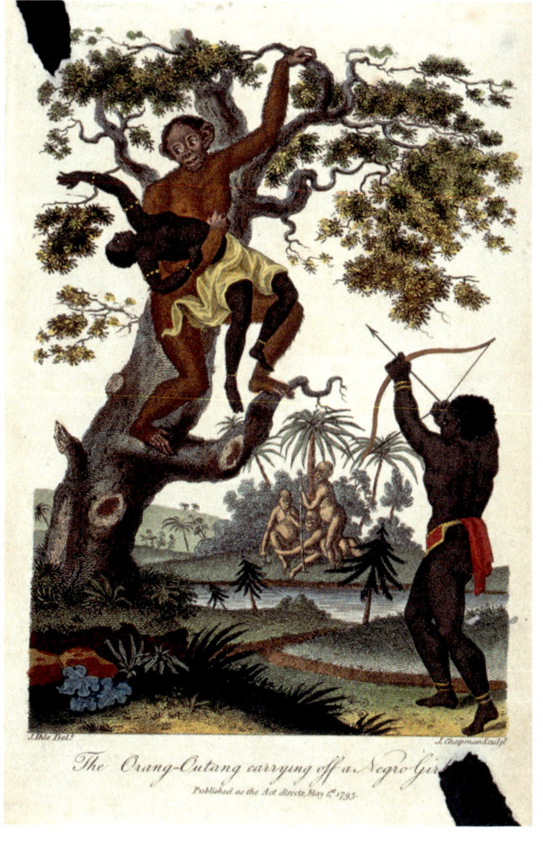

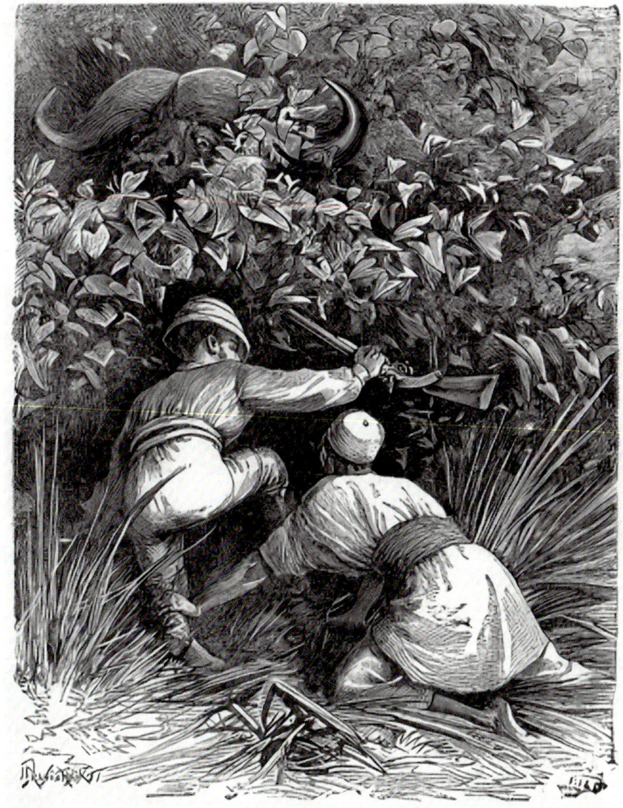

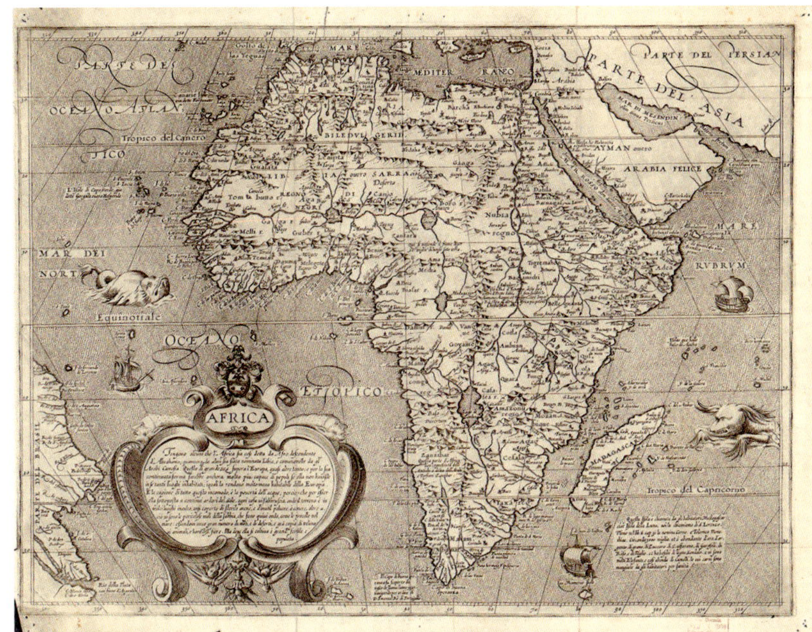

Fig. 53

Arnoldo di Arnoldi, Matteo Florimi, *Map of Africa*, ca. 1602
14 3/16 × 18 1/2 in. (36 × 47 cm)
Library of Congress, Washington, DC
Library of Congress Geography and Map Division; call # G8200 1600.A7
Library of Congress Control Number: 2005632131

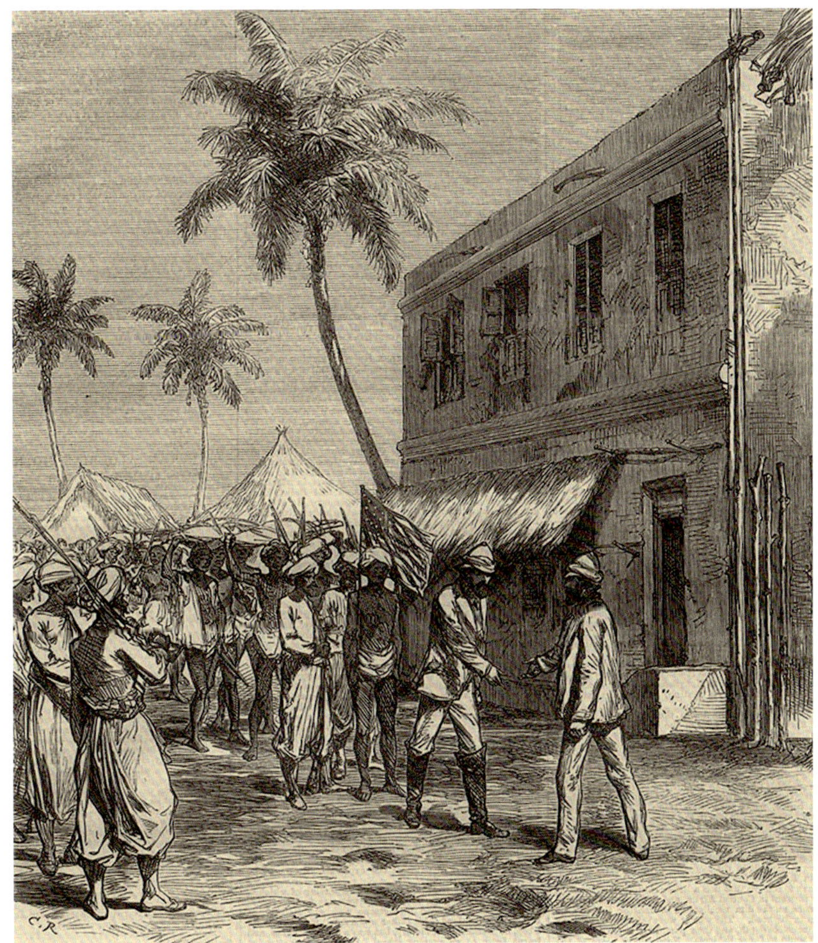

Fig. 54

Charles Robinson (fl. 1866–1878) after Lieutenant William Henn, *The Finding of Dr. Livingstone, the Return of Stanley to Bagamoyo* from a sketch by Lieutenant Henn
Illustration for *The Illustrated London News*, 3 August 1872, p. 113

to embellish their experiences to suit the Victorian public's need to project their repressed carnal fantasies onto Africa.[32] In an 1872 photo of Stanley, for example, he is posed in a London photographer's studio with fake props to approximate a jungle setting, and a child-model in rags (his adopted son Ndugu M'Hali), intended to make the scene look more rustic than Stanley's experience had actually been (fig. 56). According to Dr. Livingstone, Stanley traveled in the lap of luxury with "bales of goods, baths of tin, huge kettles, cooking-pots, tents, etc.," causing Livingstone to write, "This is one luxurious traveler."[33]

The racial and civil vanity that spurred trans-Atlantic exploration also bolstered the European need to dominate Africa, whose people were portrayed as mindless brutes, usually naked and often sexually charged (fig. 57). Artists began to place emphasis on wanton rituals, barbaric behavior, brutality, and violence—the very activities of Europeans in their successful attempts to conquer the land and people of Africa (fig. 58). The more ruthless the actions of the European "conquerors," the more savagely Africans themselves were portrayed (fig. 59). Meanwhile, colonial Europeans conveniently overlooked the fact that

Fig. 55

BOTTOM, LEFT

H. Rider Haggard, cover of *King Solomon's Mines*, 1952
Illustrated Classics #97
Classics Illustrated no. 87, King Solomon's Mines, cover art by Henry C. Kiefer, © First Classics, Inc., classicsillustratedbooks.com

Fig. 56

BOTTOM, RIGHT

London Stereoscopic & Photographic Company, *Sir Henry Morton Stanley and Ndugu M'Hali or Kalulu*, an African personal servant and adopted child of the explorer and journalist Henry Morton Stanley; carte-de-visite, 1872
4 x 2½ in. (10.2 x 6.3 cm)
Stanley, a newspaper reporter, was hired by the *New York Herald* to find Dr. Livingstone in 1872

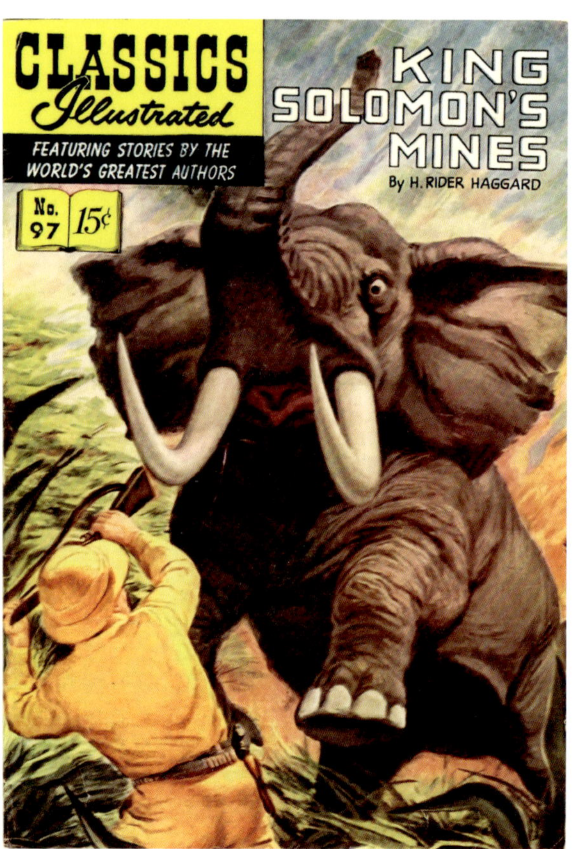

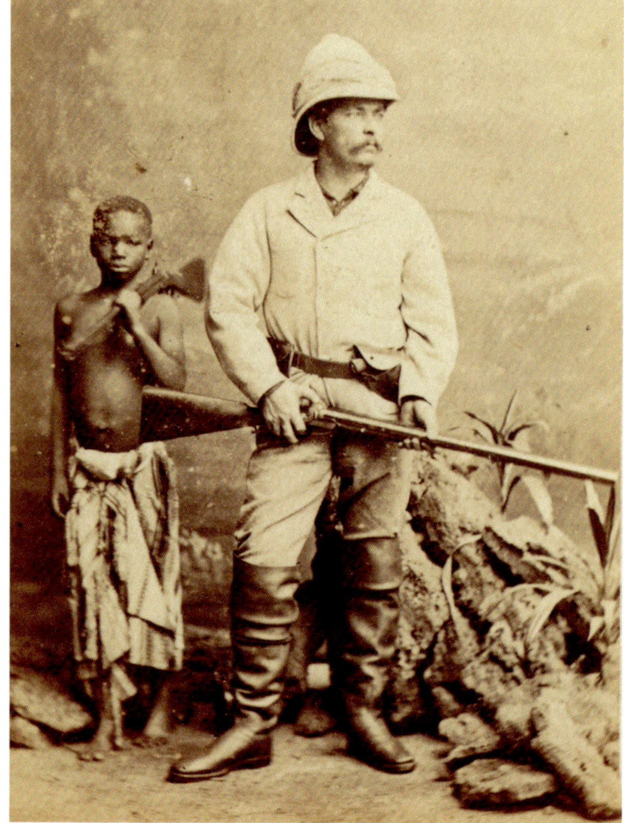

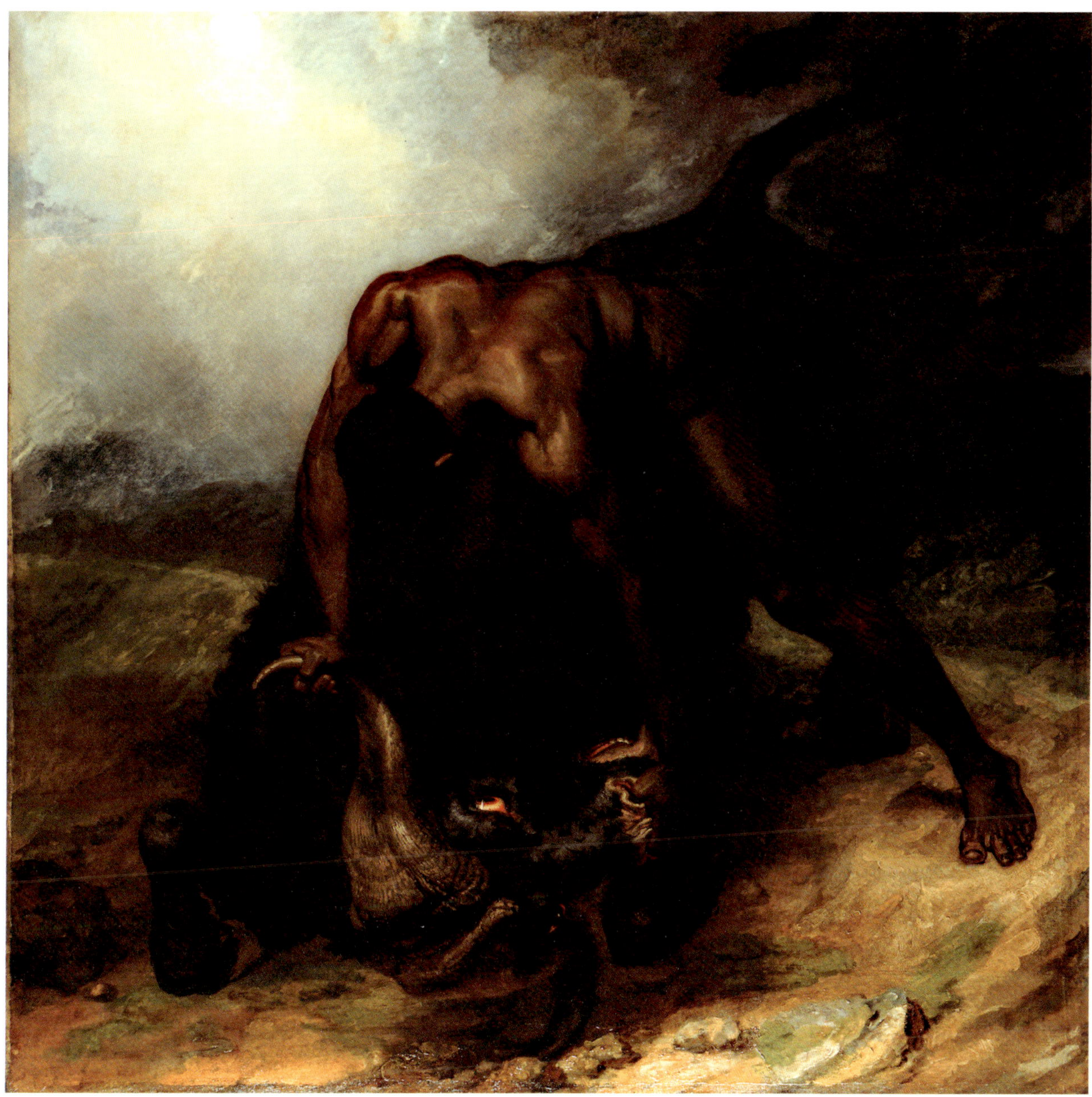

Fig. 57

George Dawe (English, 1781–1829), *A Negro Over-Powering a Buffalo: A Fact Which Occurred in America in 1809*, 1810
Oil on canvas
80 1/4 × 80 1/2 in. (203.8 × 204.5 cm).
The Menil Collection, Houston, TX
Acc. no. 1984-54 DJ

much of the violence attributed to Africans was carried out in defense of their homes. In art of eighteenth- and nineteenth-century Europe, images of African elders, dignitaries, and other authority figures began to be excluded from visual culture or replaced with exaggerated caricatures. Compare, for example, two illustrations of the Zulu King Cetshwayo. An 1879 image that appeared in the British magazine *Judy* portrays Cetshwayo

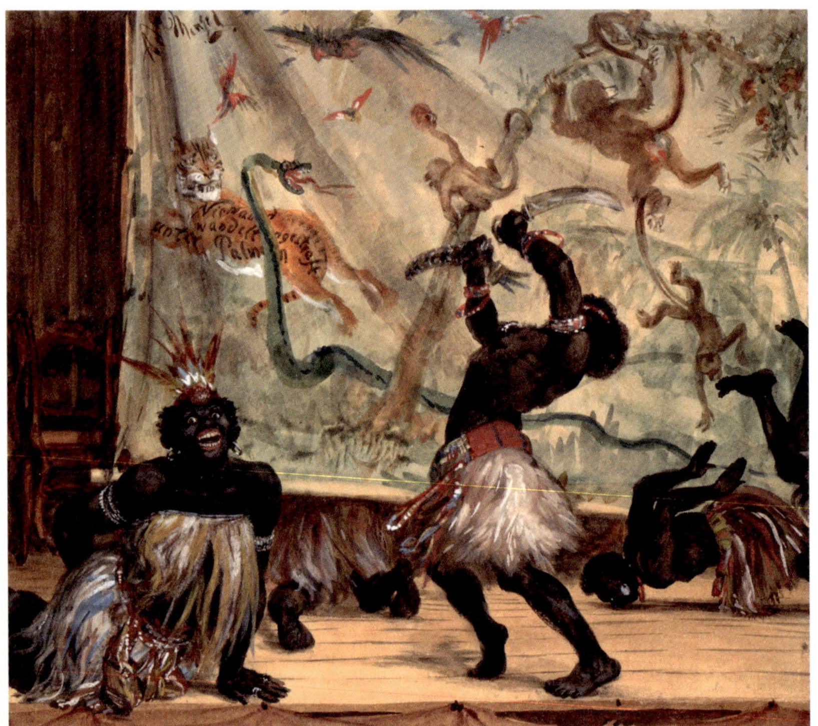

Fig. 58

Adolph Menzel (German, 1815–1905), *The Zulus*, ca. 1850
Watercolor and gouache on paper
$10\frac{13}{16} \times 11\frac{15}{16}$ in. (27.5 × 30.3 cm)
Collection of the Hamburger Kunsthalle, Hamburg, Germany
Photograph courtesy of Bridgeman Images, New York, NY

Fig. 59

Alfred Pearse (English, 1855–1933), illustrator, *Ambush at River Intombi*, from *The Pictorial World* (Hill London, May 3, 1879)
British Library, London, UK
Photograph courtesy of Bridgeman Images, Brooklyn, NY

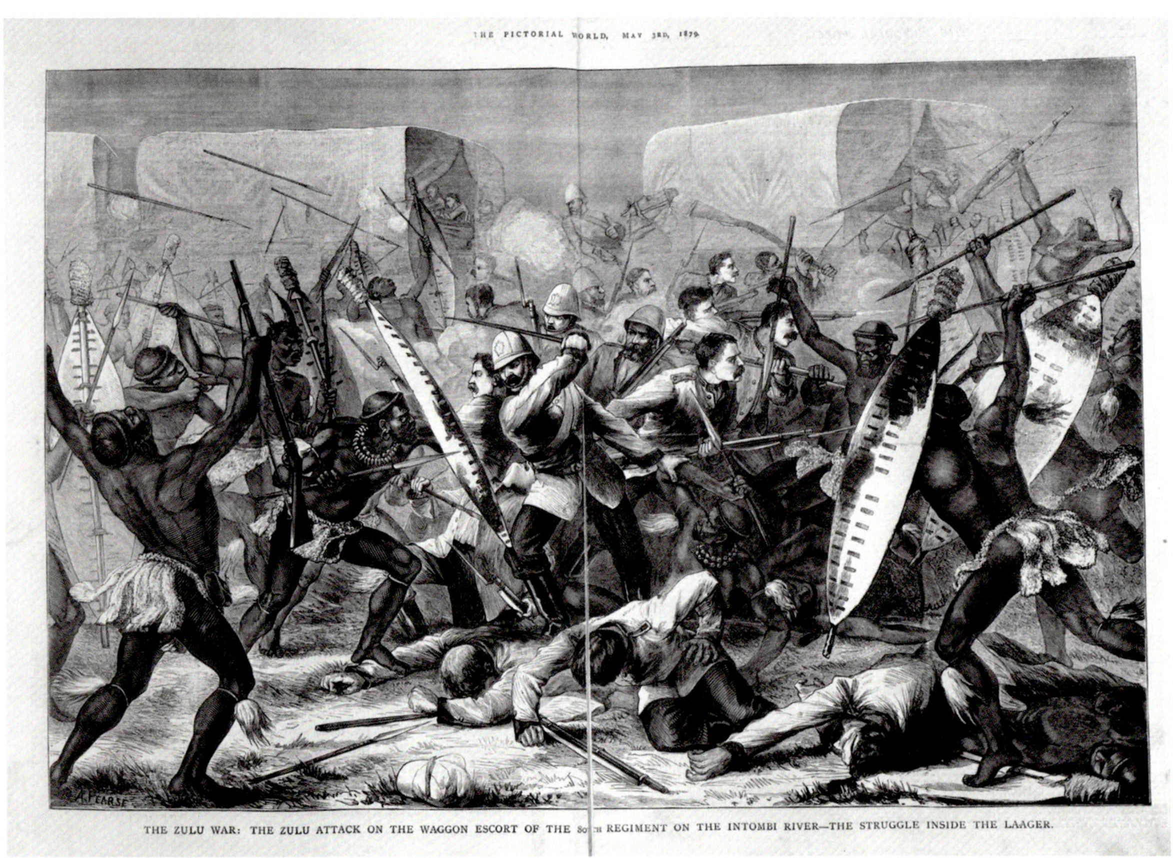

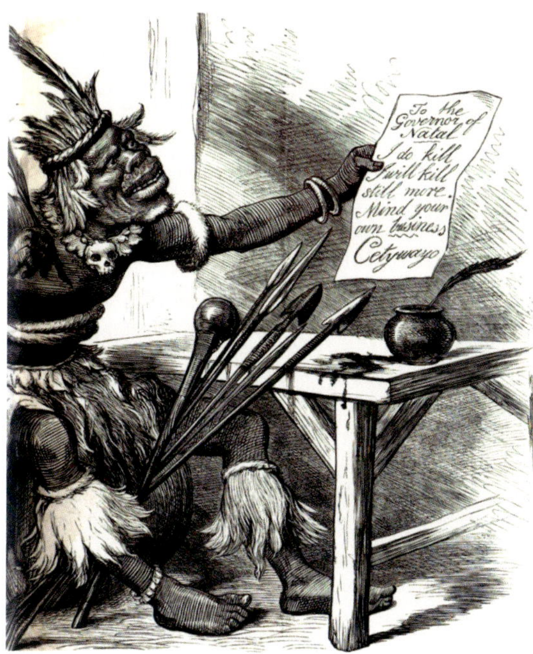

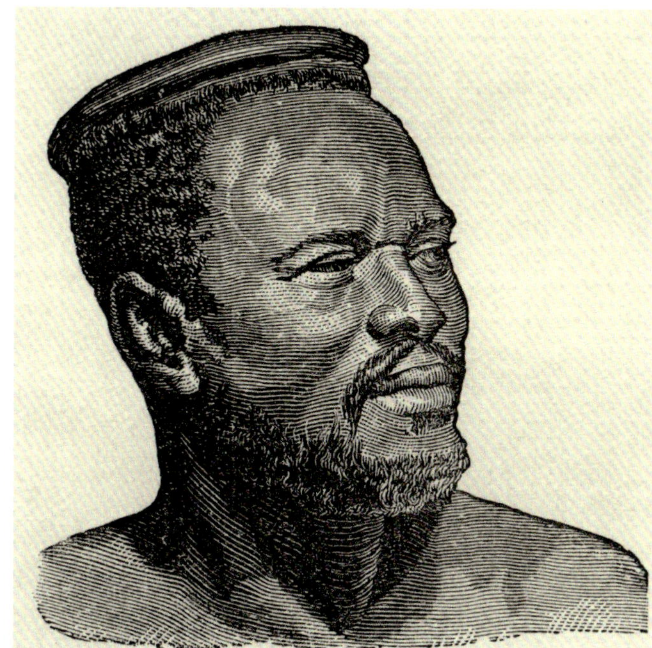

Fig. 60
LEFT
Initialed WB, *A Lesson in Diplomacy of a Certain Sort* (detail), *Judy: the London Serio-Comic Journal* (Feb 26, 1879), pp. 90–91

Fig. 61
RIGHT
G.T. Bettany (English, 1850–1891), *Cetshwayo kaMpande*, king of the Zulu nation from 1872 to 1879 and its leader during the Anglo-Zulu War in 1879; from *The World's Inhabitants* published by Ward, Lock & Co., London, UK, 1888

as a crude barbarian with coarsely exaggerated features (fig. 60). It contrasts severely with an actual portrait of the king that was intended for an anthropological text (fig. 61). The second work shows a sensitive, attractive, and intelligent man whose face and demeanor bear no resemblance to the cartoon.

Architects of Racism: Eighteenth and Nineteenth Centuries

In the second half of the eighteenth century, several respected European scholars began to engage in the pseudo-science of racial superiority and inferiority in order to prove the sub-human status of Africans and to justify European aggression against them. These men (few of whom conducted research in Africa and several of whom never met an African) were uniquely responsible for the widespread acceptance of racist theories as truth. Swedish botanist Carolus Linnaeus (fig. 62) began the onslaught with his published account in 1758 of the so-called "homo africanus," whom he described as phlegmatic or without feelings, lax, careless, crafty, and slothful or lazy with an apelike nose, swollen lips, and a desire to be ruled by authority.[34] Not surprisingly, these very same words had been used previously to describe Slavic people during the Middle Ages. Linnaeus concluded that Europeans, on the other hand, were "White skinned, blond haired, blue eyed, sanguine (or ruddy), highly intelligent, discoverers, and ruled by religious authority."[35] In other words, Africans needed to be ruled by Europeans, but Europeans could only be ruled by God and had an innate right to "discover" or conquer others' lands.

Scottish philosopher, economist, and historian David Hume (1711–1776; fig. 63) argued in his 1742 essay, "Of National Characters," that not only Africans, but "all other species of men" were inferior to Whites. He insisted that "there never was a civilized nation of any other complexion than White" and, despite historical evidence to the contrary, that Africans had produced no cultural artifacts nor made any worthy contributions to society.[36] Between 1775 and 1806, German scholar Johann Blumenbach (fig. 64) coined the term "Caucasian" after Noah's Ark, which landed in the Caucasus mountains (bordering Europe and Asia). Blumenbach described Caucasians as having "in general the kind of appearance which, according to our opinion of symmetry, we consider most handsome and becoming." Blumenbach reserved derogatory terms such as "knotty," "uneven," "puffy," and "bandy-legged" (bowlegged) for Africans. After finally meeting Africans later in his life, he couldn't reconcile them with his own descriptions, and he became a great admirer of Africans.[37]

In 1791, the son of Dutch anatomy professor Pieter (or Petrus) Camper, Adriaan Gilles Camper, published his father's sketches of skull measurements of humans and animals (fig. 65), which were used later by French zoologist Georges Cuvier (who performed the autopsy on the infamous Hottentot Venus Sarah [Saartjie] Baartman[38]) to prove the ideal beauty of Europeans versus Africans and other ethnic groups (fig. 66).[39] Georges-Louis Leclerc de Buffon (fig. 67), in one of the most widely read academic texts of the nineteenth century—the 1819 *Natural History of the Human Species* (fig. 68)—gave human beings biological hierarchies with Africans at the bottom and he described them as being as "ugly as monkeys."[40] And the German philosopher Hegel (fig. 69) lectured in 1830 that Africans were "wild and untamed in nature,"

Fig. 62

LEFT

Alexander Roslin (Swedish, 1718–1793), *Carl von Linné / Carl Linnaeus*, 1775
Oil on canvas
22 x 18⅛ in. (56 cm x 46 cm)
The National Portrait Gallery of Sweden, Mariefred, Sweden
Acc. no. NMGrh 1053

Fig. 63

CENTER

Allan Ramsay (Scottish, 1713–1784), *David Hume*, 1766
Oil on canvas
30 x 25 in. (76.2 x 63.5 cm)
The National Galleries of Scotland, Edinburgh, Scotland
Acc. no. PG 1057

Fig. 64

RIGHT

Johann Elias Haid (German, 1739–1809), *Johann Friedrich Blumenbach*, ca. 1800
Mezzotint
Wellcome Library, London, UK
Wellcome Images, images@wellcome.ac.uk

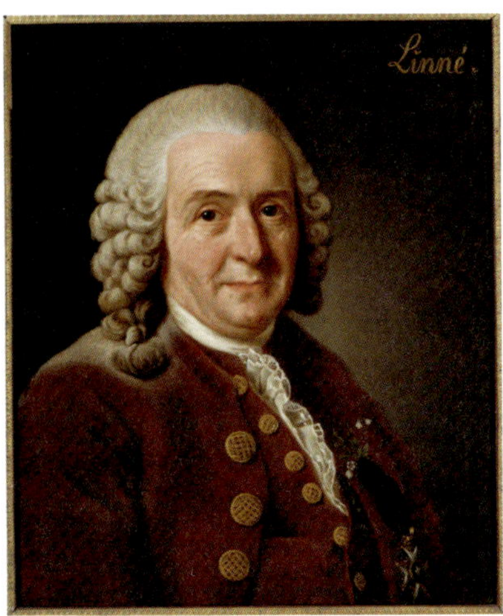

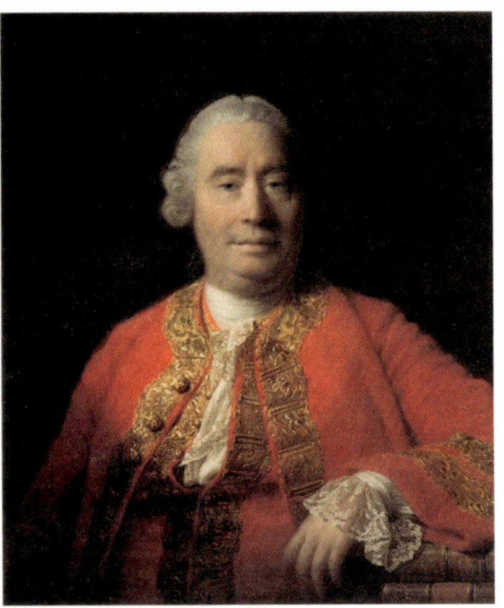

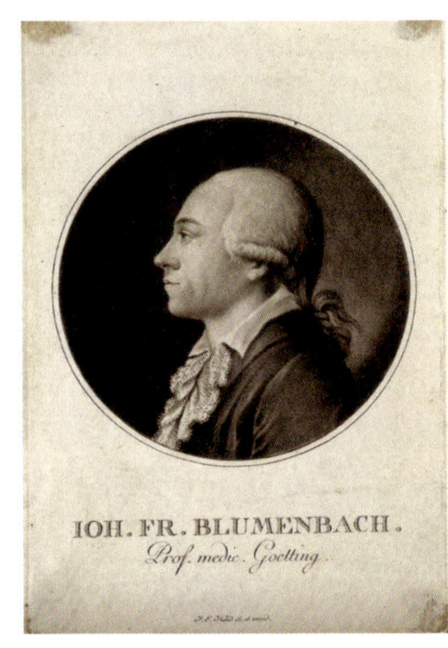

Fig. 65

TOP

The Works of the late Professor Camper, on The Connexion [sic] between the Science of Anatomy and The Arts of Drawing, Painting, Statuary &c. &c., 1794
Etched or engraved illustration
$12\frac{3}{8} \times 9\frac{13}{16} \times 1\frac{3}{16}$ in.
(31.5 x 25 x 3 cm)
The Metropolitan Museum of Art, New York, NY
The Elisha Whittelsey Collection, The Elisha Whittelsey Fund, 1960; 60.511.1

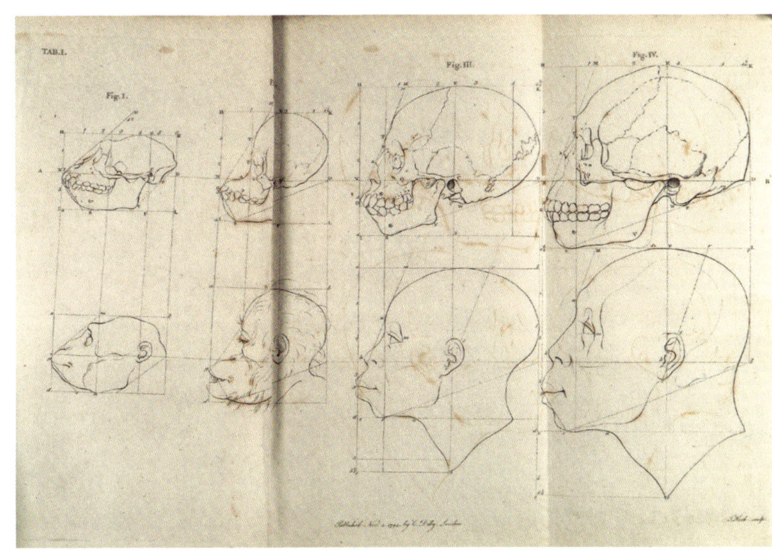

Fig. 66

MIDDLE, LEFT

James Thomson (British, 1788–1850), *Portrait of Georges Cuvier*, 1833
Engraving published by Charles Knight from an original drawing in the possession of the Baroness Cuvier, Paris
Smithsonian Libraries, Washington, DC; image ID: SIL-SIL14-C6-10, Photograph courtesy of Wikimedia Commons

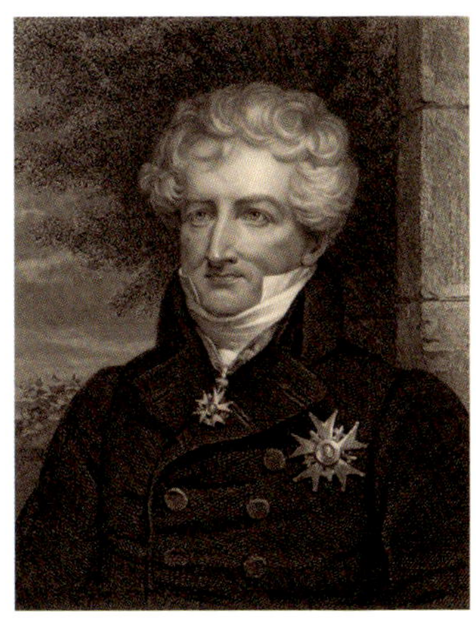

Fig. 67

MIDDLE, RIGHT

Thomas Hart (British, 1776–?), *Portrait of Georges Louis Leclerc de Buffon*, eighteenth-century engraving after François Hubert Drouais, published by William Mackenzie

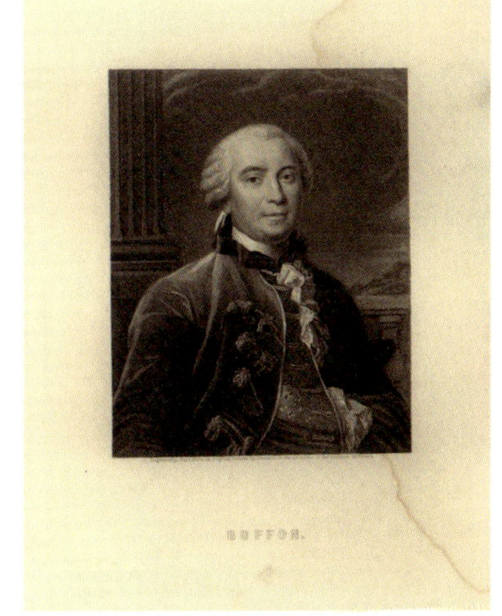

Fig. 68

BOTTOM, LEFT

Title page of Georges Louis Leclerc Buffon's *Histoire naturelle, generale et particuliere, avec la description du cabinet du roy*, vol. 1, (Paris: De l'Imprimerie Royale, 1749)

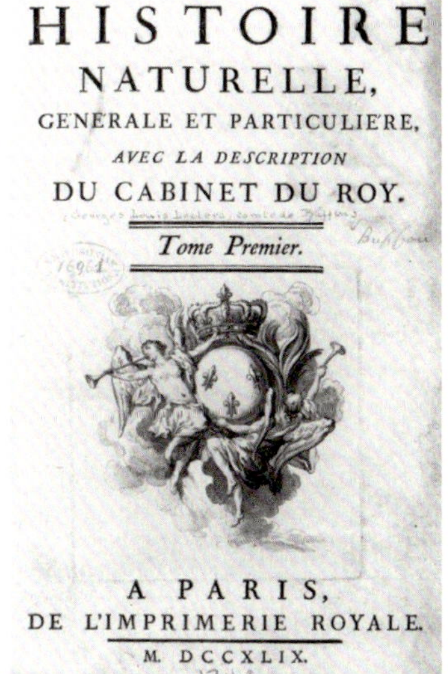

HISTOIRE
NATURELLE,
GENERALE ET PARTICULIERE,
AVEC LA DESCRIPTION
DU CABINET DU ROY.
Tome Premier.

A PARIS,
DE L'IMPRIMERIE ROYALE.
M. DCCXLIX.

Fig. 69

BOTTOM, RIGHT

Jacob Schlesinger (German, 1792–1855), *Portrait of Georg Wilhelm Friedrich Hegel*, 1831
Oil on canvas
$14\frac{1}{8} \times 11\frac{5}{16}$ in. (36 x 28.8 cm)
Collection of Alte Nationalgalerie, Staatliche Museen zu Berlin, Berlin, Germany

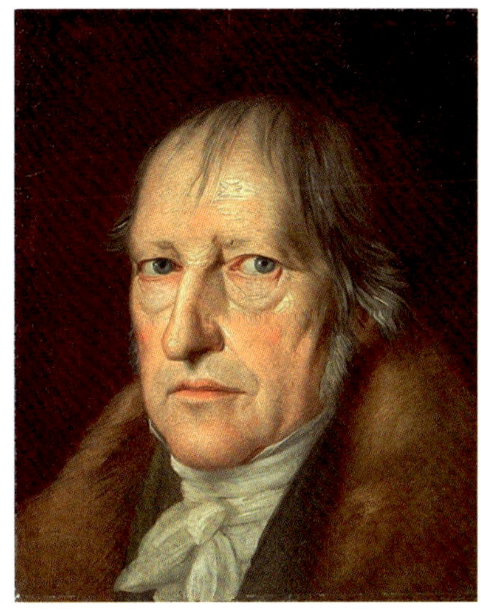

bereft of "morality and sensitivity," and had "nothing remotely human" in their character.[41]

Finally, sealing the coffin on this century-long scientific campaign against Blacks, Charles Darwin's much cited *On the Origin of Species* was published in 1859 (figs. 70, 71).[42] Contrary to popular belief, however, it did not malign Africans; in fact, it hardly mentions them. When Darwin does discuss race in his much later 1871 *Descent of Man* (fig. 72), a substantially lesser-known book, he admits in chapters 7 and 9 to having been "incessantly struck, after meeting Africans in South America, with the many little traits of character showing how similar their minds were to Europeans; and so it was the same," he said, "with a full-blooded African whom [he] happened once to meet."[43] Again, like so many other racial theorists of the time, by his own admission, Darwin had almost no meaningful contact with Black Africans.[44] More important than this is the fact that nowhere in Darwin's *On the Origin of Species* does he use the term "survival of the fittest," but rather, he repeatedly argues for the survival of the most adaptable.

In his chapter on natural selection, Darwin states that extinction is a result of natural selection. For example, if climate changes occur, inhabitants must quickly adapt or become extinct. In his words, "Those who best adapt to altered conditions will survive and improve." He goes on to say that Man's selection—that is, human beings' decisions as to who will live and who will die—is inferior to natural selection because Man bases his selection on superficial visible characteristics (like skin color) rather than on internal biological ones. In Darwin's words, "Nature cares nothing for appearances. . . . How fleeting are the wishes and efforts of man! how short his time!

Fig. 70
LEFT

Julia Magaret Cameron (British, 1815–1879), *Charles Darwin*, ca. 1868
Halftone photograph
The Library of Congress Prints and Photographs Division Washington, DC
Repro. no. LC-USZ62-11954 USA

Fig. 71
CENTER

Title page from Charles Darwin, *On the Origin of Species by Means of Natural Selection* (London: John Murray, 1859)

Fig. 72
RIGHT

Title page from Charles Darwin, *The Descent of Man and Selection in Relation to Sex* (London: John Murray, 1871)

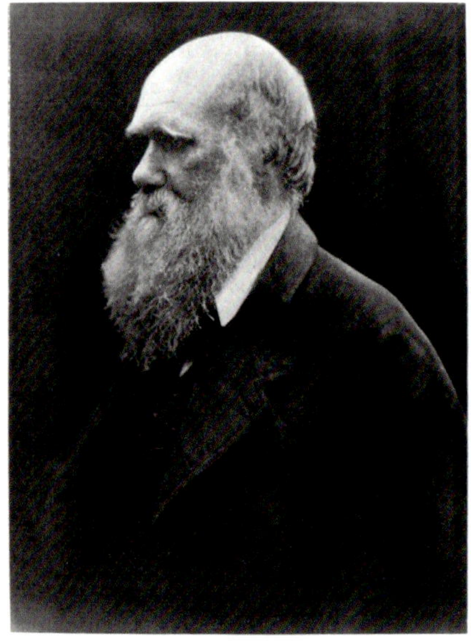

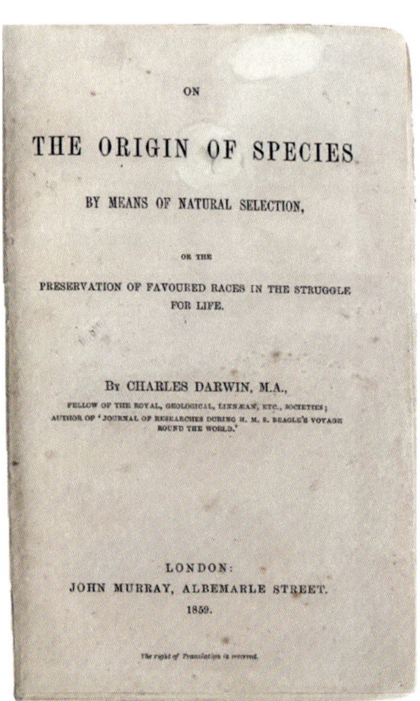

ON

THE ORIGIN OF SPECIES

BY MEANS OF NATURAL SELECTION,

OR THE

PRESERVATION OF FAVOURED RACES IN THE STRUGGLE FOR LIFE.

BY CHARLES DARWIN, M.A.,

FELLOW OF THE ROYAL, GEOLOGICAL, LINNÆAN, ETC., SOCIETIES; AUTHOR OF 'JOURNAL OF RESEARCHES DURING H. M. S. BEAGLE'S VOYAGE ROUND THE WORLD.'

LONDON:
JOHN MURRAY, ALBEMARLE STREET.
1859.

The right of Translation is reserved.

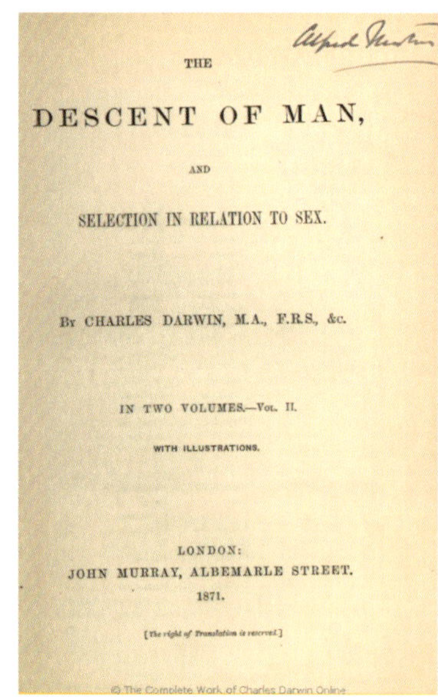

THE

DESCENT OF MAN,

AND

SELECTION IN RELATION TO SEX.

BY CHARLES DARWIN, M.A., F.R.S., &c.

IN TWO VOLUMES.—VOL. II.

WITH ILLUSTRATIONS.

LONDON:
JOHN MURRAY, ALBEMARLE STREET.
1871.

[*The right of Translation is reserved.*]

And consequently, how poor his selections will be compared to those of Nature. . . ."[45]

About sexual selection, Darwin argues that it is "not a struggle for existence but a struggle between males for possession of the females. The result is not death to the unsuccessful competitor but few or no offspring. The most vigorous males will leave the most progeny,"[46] suggesting that a basic primal fear of extinction motivates fears of interracial sexual exchange. Darwin was in favor of cross-fertilization; he wrote that "Inter-fertilization within a species results in a gain in vigor and fertility . . . " whereas, self-fertilization (or the perpetuation of so-called genetic "purity") results in less chance of survival and propagation, and leads to rarity, which, as Darwin describes, "is a direct precursor to extinction because rare species adapt slowly and will consequently be beaten in the race for life by more adaptable, commoner species. . . . The more diversified a group's descendants become, the better their chance of succeeding in the battle for life."[47] If applied to humans (which, by the way, was not Darwin's objective), his writings suggest that the genetic characteristics of "commoner" species (such as dark skin, hair, and eyes) indicate the highest probability of survival.

So, the question is, how have we come to know Darwin's texts as the basis for racism? The man responsible for this feat of conjuring is the English political theorist, Herbert Spencer (fig. 73). It was he and not Darwin who coined the phrase "survival of the fittest" in his *Principles of Biology*, first published in 1864.[48] In this book, where he misapplied Darwin's scientific theories to political and social theory, Spencer insisted that those who had accrued the most economic and political power since the Industrial Revolution were the most worthy and likely to survive, rather than, as Darwin believed, those who were most adaptable to environmental change. In this notorious secondary- (rather than primary-) source document, Spencer managed to twist the meaning of Darwin's research so as to justify European colonial aggression.

Fig. 73

John Bagnold Burgess, photograph of Herbert Spencer, 1896
Photograph courtesy of Wikimedia Commons

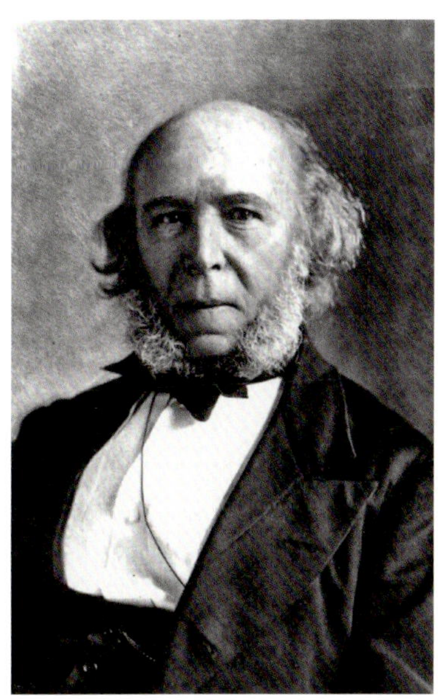

The result of relying solely on secondary sources for information is often misinformation or some form of distortion that reflects not so much the content and intent of the primary-source material, but rather the agenda of the interpreter of that material—the author of the secondary source. Spencer's intent was, evidently, to justify the economic ascendancy of Europe since the Industrial Revolution by suggesting that non-Europeans were biologically unfit to wield power. Darwin had no such agenda. Unfortunately, the Darwin/Spencer dichotomy is not unique. In the main, the written texts from which most of us gain knowledge qualify as secondary sources because they are interpretations, reinterpretations, translations, or reconfigurations of other primary-source texts. One might equate the "reading" of a secondary source to the experience of watching the remake of a movie, or the film adaptation of a novel. Without having seen the initial film or read the original book, one has no idea what or how much the author of the secondary source may have added to, deleted from, or modified the primary one. Spencer, who wrote mostly about political theory, is referred to as the father of "Social Darwinism" and his theories are today widely criticized as "scientism"—that is, the misapplication of science to fields unsuitable for it. Sadly, most nineteenth century readers gleaned what they knew of Darwin from Spencer's nonscientific writings.

Reinforced by a newly unearthed fifth-century Talmudic reference to the descendants of Noah's son Ham (cursed by God to become a slave) as being "dark" in appearance, the widely publicized biases of eighteenth- and nineteenth-century European scholars changed the course of history and convinced the population of the entire globe that Africans were less than human.[49] Scholars today rightly debunk the "Black Ham" theory as a justification for slavery, most significantly because the primary-source biblical text mentions neither the race nor the skin color of Ham nor his descendants.[50] Nevertheless, the bigoted outlooks of these colonial-era European intellectuals stand in stark contrast to earlier descriptions, such as one written by a Franciscan Friar in 1350 which described Africans as "men of intelligence with good brains . . . understanding and knowledge" (fig. 74).[51] Their chauvinism belied the sensitive

Fig. 74

Jan Jansz Mostaert (Dutch, 1475–1555), *Portrait of an African Nobleman*, ca. 1525–1530
Oil on panel
12 1/8 × 8 3/8 in. (30.8 × 21.2 cm)
Rijksmuseum, Amsterdam, Netherlands

Fig. 75

Albrecht Dürer (German, 1471–1528), *Portrait of African Woman Catherine (Porträt der Afrikanerin Katherina)*, 1521
Silverpoint drawing on paper
7 7/8 × 5 1/2 in. (20 × 14 cm)
The Uffizi Gallery, Florence, Italy

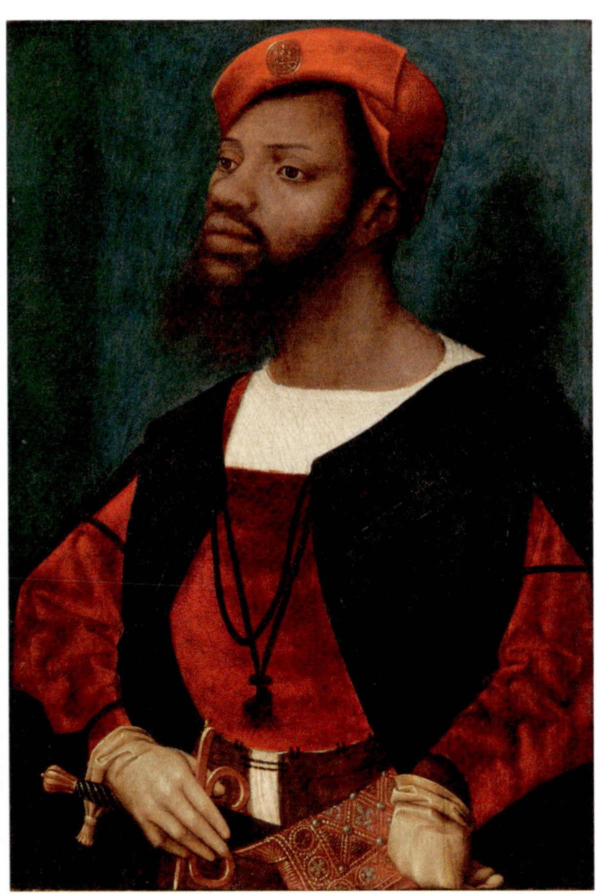

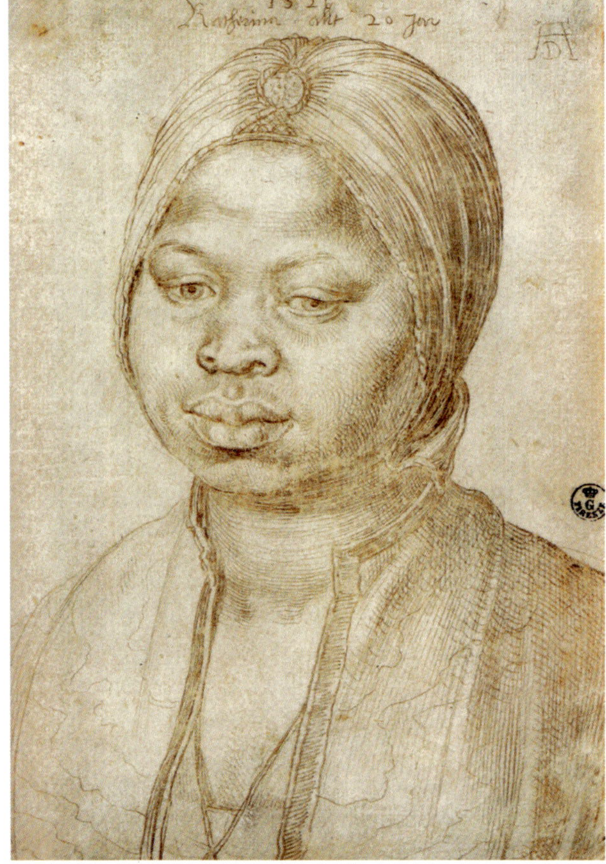

and dignified depictions of Africans who had lived in Europe for centuries, such as a Moorish woman named Catherine, sketched by German Renaissance master Albrecht Dürer in 1521 (fig. 75), or the 1610 studies of an attractive Belgian African by Baroque virtuoso Peter Paul Rubens (fig. 76). The celebrated Dutch painter Rembrandt portrayed two Black Europeans in classical Roman-inspired military clothing in 1661 (fig. 77), and Spanish master Diego Velázquez painted a sympathetic and penetrating portrait of his Moorish assistant, Juan de Pareja, who was an artist in his own right and a favorite of the Spanish king (fig. 78). Even as late as 1797, African diplomats, such as Jean-Baptiste Belley, 1793 French National Convention member, were the distinguished subjects of portraits by French academic painters (p. 20). The visual-art primary sources available to us make it clear that Europeans and Africans were ready friends, shared mutual admiration, and coexisted for thousands of years before the onset of racial theories.

Even today, most Americans have never visited Africa and limit their knowledge of Africa to peeks at the continent through the editorial filters of

Fig. 76

Peter Paul Rubens (Flemish, 1577–1640), *Four Studies of the Head of a Moor*, ca. 1614–1616
Oil on canvas transferred from wood
20 1/16 x 26 in. (51 x 66 cm)
Royal Museums of Fine Arts of Belgium, Brussels, Belgium

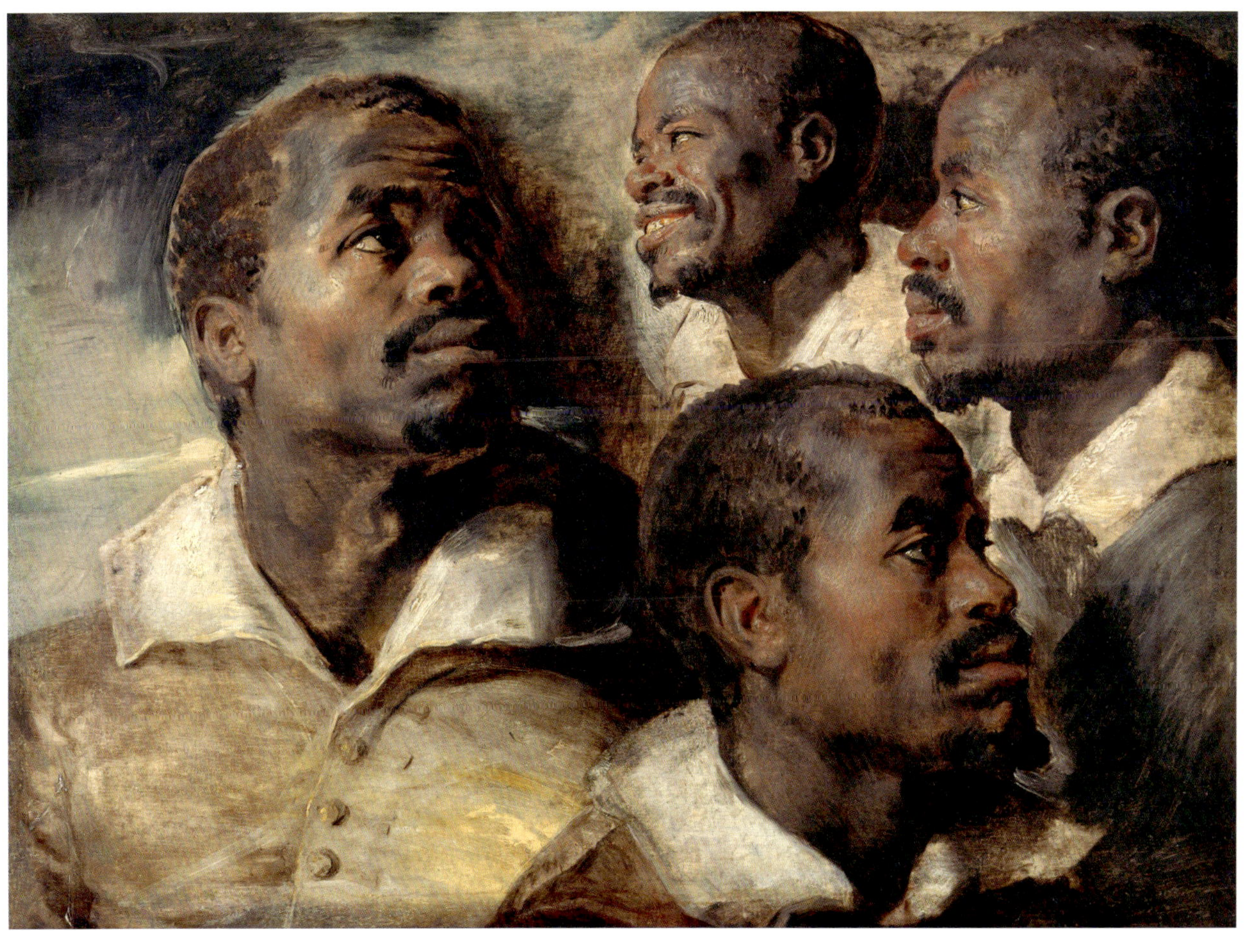

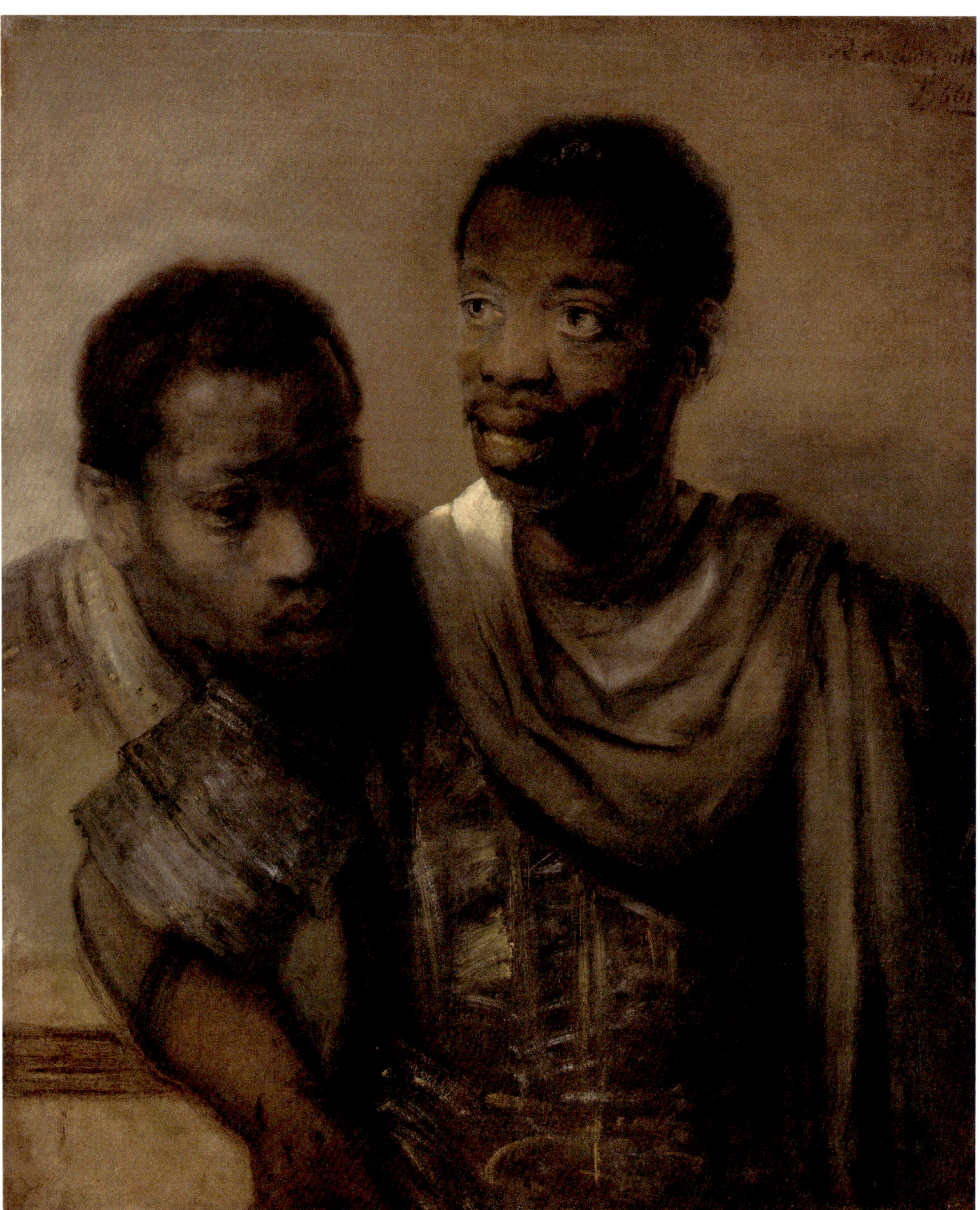

Fig. 77

OPPOSITE

Rembrandt van Rijn (Dutch, 1609–1669), *Two Africans*, 1661
Oil on canvas
30 11/16 x 25 3/16 in. (78 x 64 cm)
Collection of the Mauritshuis, The Hague, Netherlands
Inventory no. 665

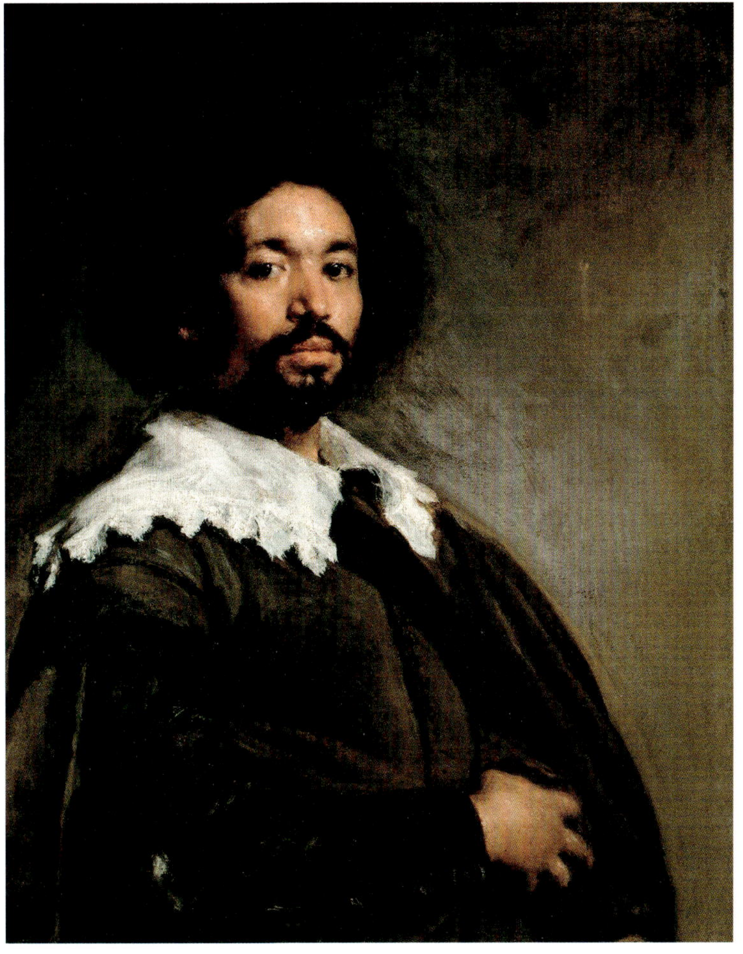

Fig. 78

RIGHT

Diego Velázquez (Spanish, 1599–1660), *Juan de Pareja*, 1650
Oil on canvas
32 x 27 1/2 in. (81.3 x 69.9 cm)
The Metropolitan Museum of Art, New York, NY
Purchase, Fletcher and Rogers Funds, and Bequest of Miss Adelaide Milton de Groot (1876–1967), by exchange, supplemented by gifts from friends of the Museum, 1971; acc. no. 1971.86

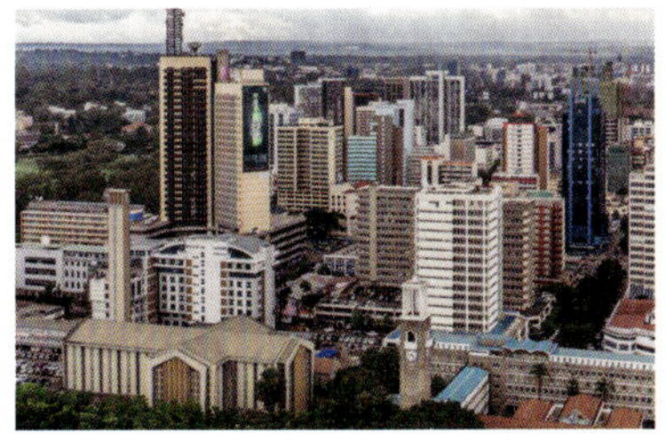

Fig. 79

Nairobi, Kenya, city center and Holy Family Basilica, photographed from the Kenyatta International Conference Centre, 2015 Photograph courtesy of Wikimedia Commons / Ninara at https://www.flickr.com/photos/ninara/17297660486/

the film industry, the news media, museums, *Smithsonian Magazine, National Geographic* or the Discovery Channel. Many Americans have little, if any, knowledge of the metropolitan skylines of Africa's cities such as Dakar and, Bamako, Accra and Abuja, Nairobi (fig. 79) or Dar Es Salaam. As is evident in eighteenth- and nineteenth-century works of art by renowned European artists such as Reynolds, Copley, Cordier, and Deutsch among many others (figs. 80–83), it is vital that we make the choice to discover the world and its history on our own, rather than allowing others to spoon feed it to us in murky bites. We must commit to consulting primary sources rather than secondary ones, or we risk knowing little, if anything, of the truth of our past. Primary sources, such as those discussed herein, are invaluable not only because they help to unveil an obscured history, but because they offer us hope. They offer a fresh and optimistic look at the human condition and at race relations, and they have the potential to guide us to a place that is far more humane than the one in which we have lived for so long.

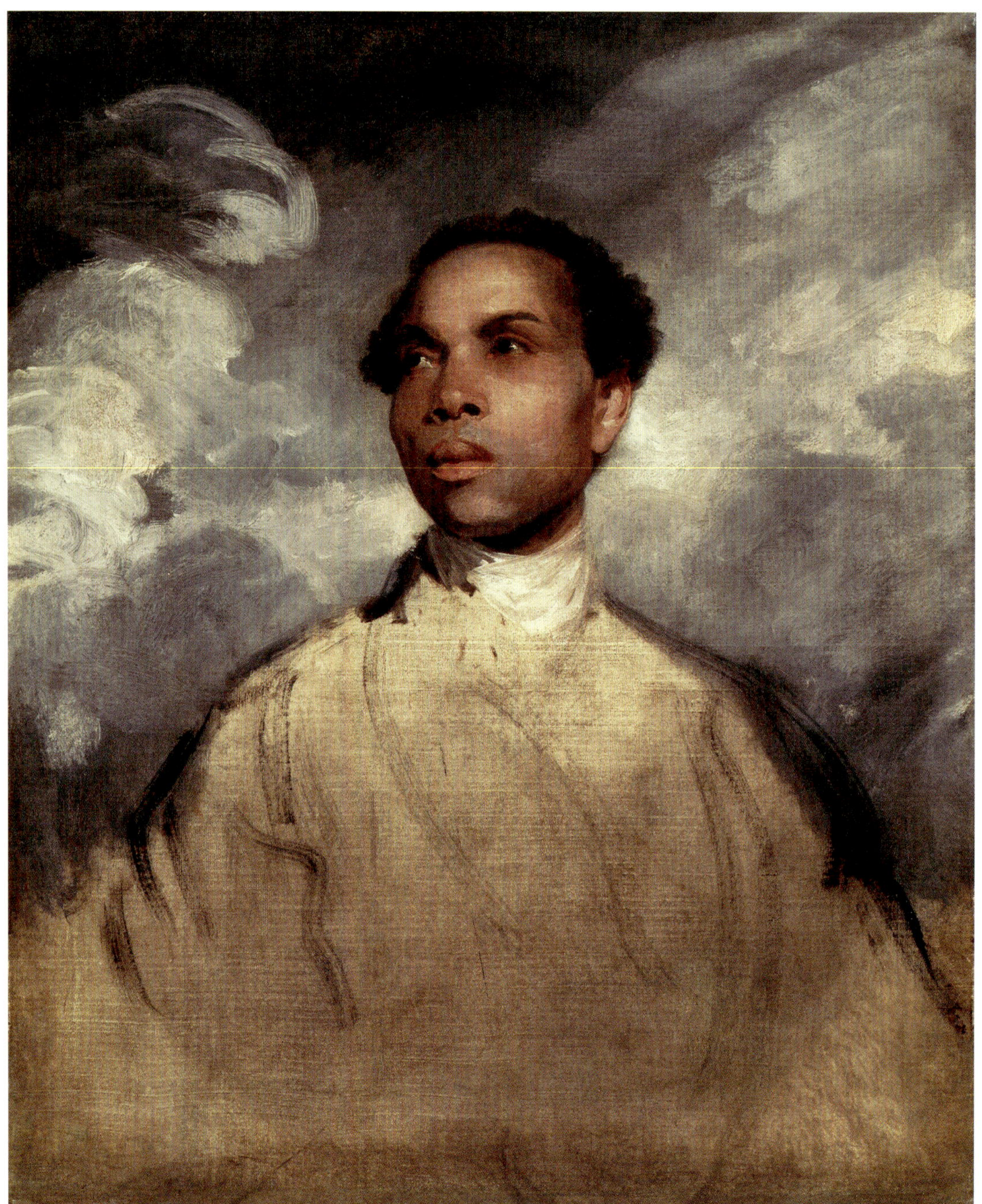

Fig. 80

Sir Joshua Reynolds (British, 1723–1792), *Portrait of a Man, probably Francis Barber*, ca. 1770
Oil on canvas
31 × 25 1/8 in. (78.7 × 63.8 cm)
The Menil Collection, Houston, TX; acc. no. 1983-103 DJ

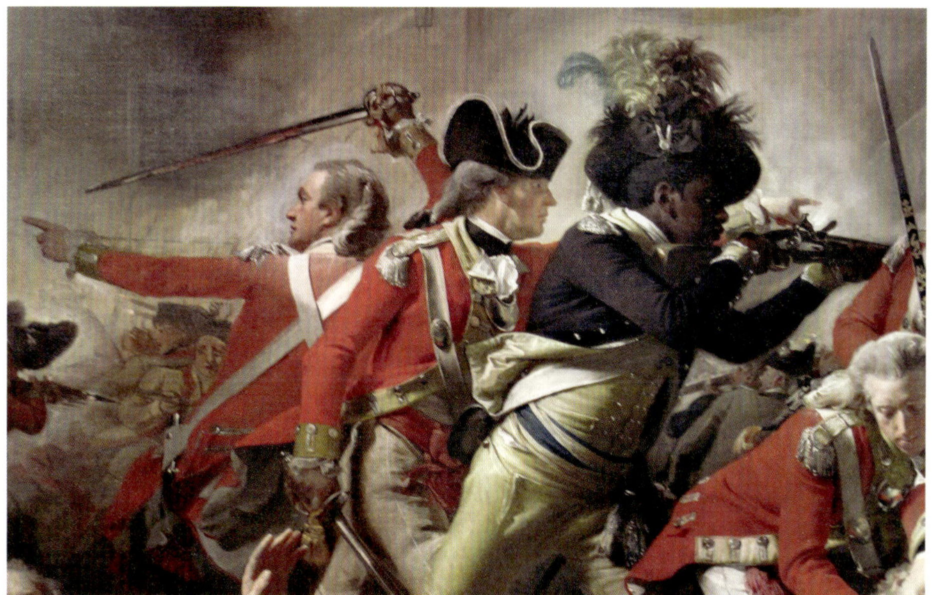

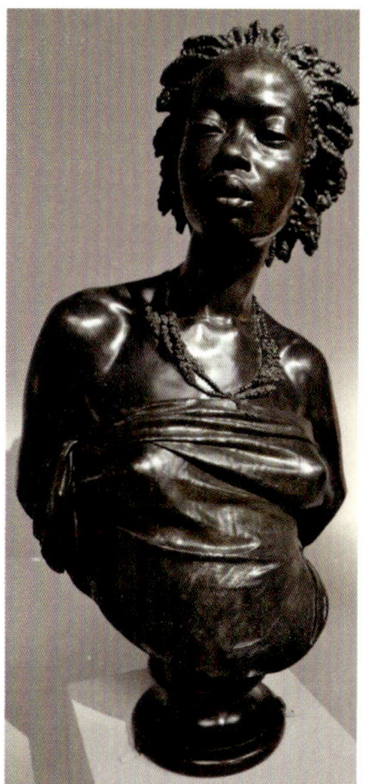

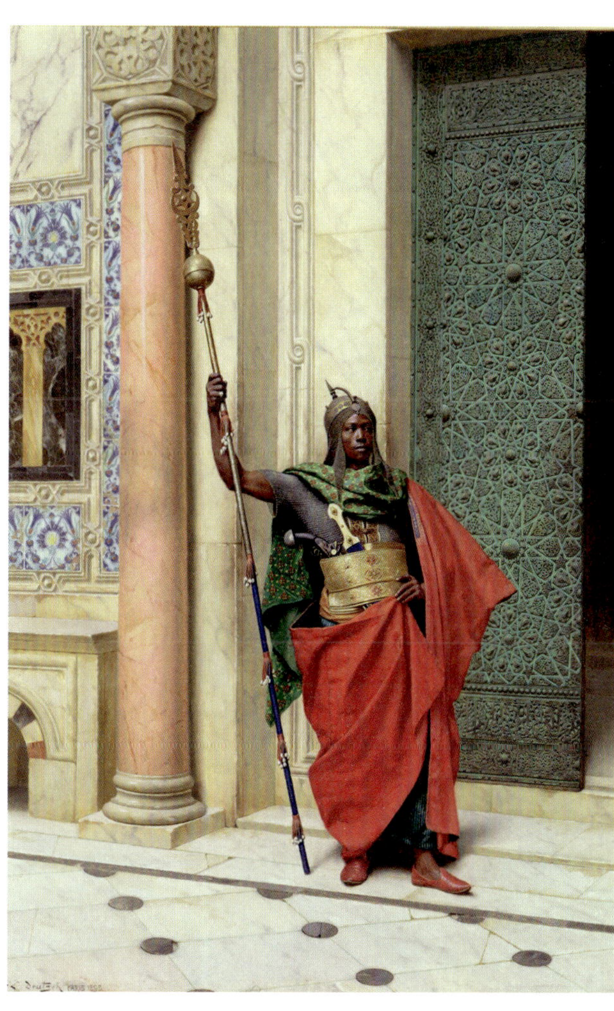

Fig. 81

TOP, LEFT

John Singleton Copley (Anglo American, 1738–1815), *The Death of Major Peirson, 6 January 1781*, 1783 (detail)
Oil on canvas
99 x 144 in. (251.4 x 365.8 cm)
Collection of the Tate Gallery, London, UK, ref. no. N00733

Fig. 82

TOP, RIGHT

Charles Henri Joseph Cordier (French, 1827–1905), *African Venus*, 1851
Bronze
28 3⁄16 x 16 x 11 1⁄2 in.
(71.5 x 40.6 x 29.2 cm)
The Art Institute of Chicago, Chicago, IL
Ada Turnbull Hertle Endowment
Ref. no. 1963.840
Photogaph courtesy of Wikimedia Commons

Fig. 83

Ludwig Deutsch (French Austrian, 1855–1935), *A Nubian Guard,* 1895
Oil on canvas
19 15⁄16 x 13 in. (50.5 x 33 cm)
Private collection
Photograph courtesy of Bridgeman Images, Brooklyn, NY

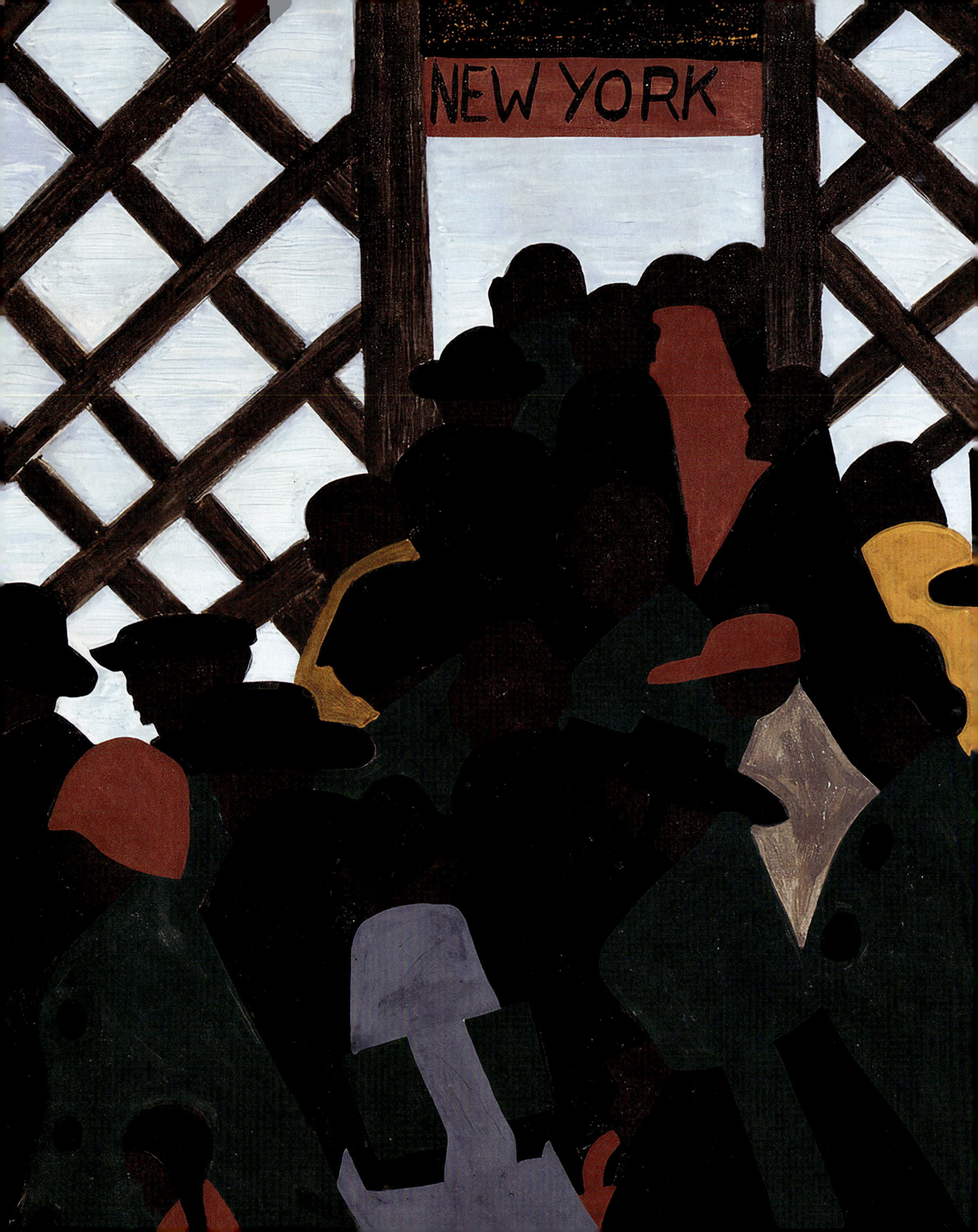
NEW YORK

Part Four: Epilogue

The Early Twentieth Century: The Harlem Renaissance

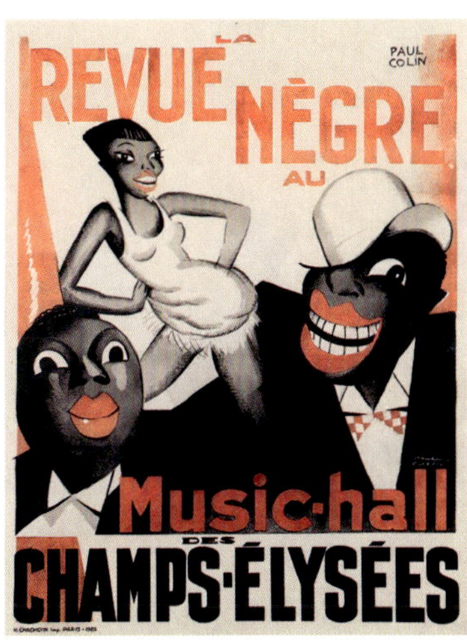

Fig. 84

Paul Colin (French, 1892–1985), *La Revue Nègre*, 1925
Poster
46⅛ x 61⅝ in. (117 x 156.5 cm)
Imp. H. Chachoin, Paris

Left

Detail of fig. 93, *Migration Series*, p. 79

Just as medieval Europeans expressed their genuine admiration for Blacks in their art, from the ages of African enslavement to the later Jim Crow era and that of apartheid (when legalized racial segregation replaced the banned practice of slavery to create a de facto state of enslavement), disdain for Blacks was expressed through persuasive, exaggerated, and distorted images of them as barbarians, primitives, sambos, and pickaninnies in art and film (fig. 84). This campaign made it virtually impossible for the world to perceive Africans in the diaspora in any holistic or unbiased way. The result was a skewed vision of Blacks filtered through the eyes of non-Blacks. The drawback of learning about Blacks (or any group) through representations created by others is that one's knowledge derives from the inherent biases of the others, for good or ill. Black artists, in their attempts to thwart distorted perceptions, concluded that the only authentic sources for information about Blacks were Blacks themselves. Because it has been established that art provides a near-foolproof form of primary-source documents, one can conceivably turn to visual imagery created by Blacks for the most accurate knowledge about how they perceive themselves. Just as we study Egyptian pyramids and monuments for insights into the ancient Egyptian psyche, Greek sculpture and architecture to understand classical Greek culture, or Gothic architecture for an understanding of medieval Europe, we study Black art to obtain accurate knowledge of Africans in the diaspora.

In the early twentieth century, Blacks began the slow and painful process of reestablishing their human status by way of art. An early and significant push in this direction occurred in 1900 in London, which hosted the first Pan-African Conference. The conference was organized by, among many, the activist and educator Booker T. Washington (fig. 85); the Haitian Ambassador to France, Benito Sylvain; and the Sierre Leone–born religious leader and activist residing in England, Bishop James Johnson. The purpose of this international gathering was to denounce and disprove theories of racial superiority; to showcase Black genius in all professions; to promote solidarity among

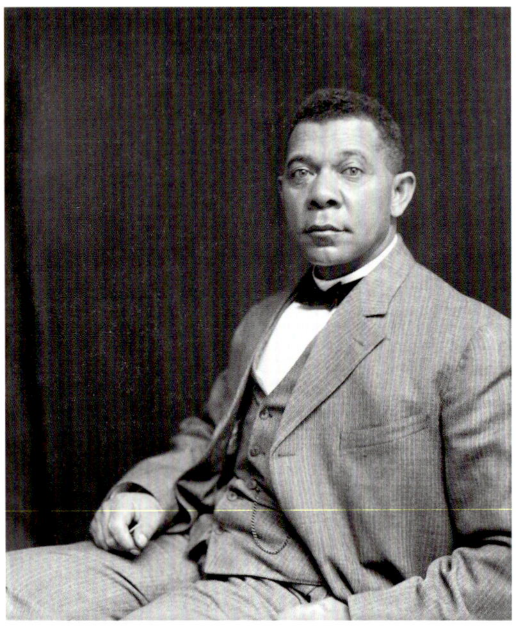

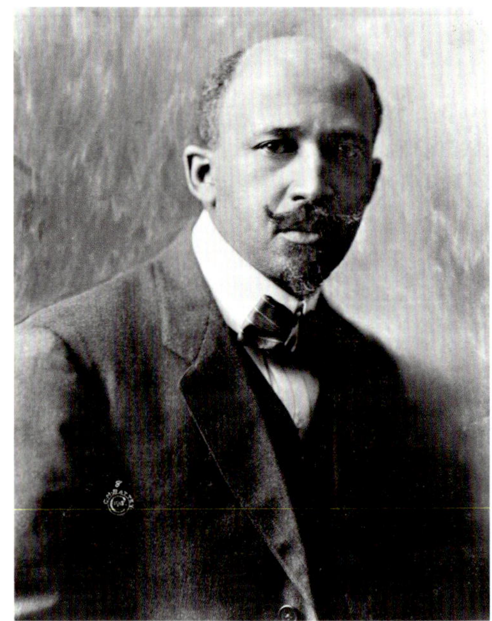

Africans globally; to combat injustice against Africans in the diaspora; and to counteract government-sanctioned racism.[52] A second Pan-African Conference was held two decades later in Paris in 1919, coincident with the Versailles Peace Conference following World War I. Orchestrated by civil rights activist and scholar W.E.B. Du Bois (fig. 86) and a Senegalese member of France's Chamber of Deputies, Blaise Diagne, the goal of the Paris conference was to put an end to international colonialism, which, like Jim Crow in America, functioned to create de facto slavery in countries around the world.[53]

In 1919, when an exhibit of paintings by the African American artist (and later French expatriate) Henry Tanner was mounted at the upscale Knoedler Gallery in New York City, it drew widespread attention to Black artistic genius. The Tanner show was followed in 1921 by a group exhibition of painting and sculpture at Harlem's 135th Street branch of the New York Public Library (today's Schomburg Center for Research in Black Culture). This show became an annual event and set the stage for the ascendency of Black visual arts. Four years later, New York City's Harlem became the nexus of the Harlem Renaissance, an interdisciplinary artistic movement, the effects of which were felt across the country and around the world.[54] At about the same time in Europe, Africa, and the Caribbean, similar movements—particularly Negritude, an anti-colonial movement of the 1930s by African and Caribbean expatriates in Paris, and Indigenism, a sister movement to Negritude centered in Haiti—were also launched.[55] Involving music, dance, theater, literature, and the visual arts, this period of cultural activity among people of African descent was unprecedented. For the first time in modern history, the interests of White art dealers, patrons, literati, critics, and curators turned toward Black art on a grand scale.

Fig. 85

LEFT

Frances Benjamin Johnston (American, 1864–1952), *Booker T. Washington*, ca. 1895
Photograph
8 x 10 in. (20.3 x 25.4 cm)
Collection of the Library of Congress, Prints and Photographs Division, Washington, DC
Source: http://hdl.loc.gov/loc.pnp/pp.print
Reproduction number: LC-J694-255
Call Number: LC-J694-255

Fig. 86

RIGHT

W.E.B. (William Edward Burghardt) Du Bois, 1868–1963
Collection of the Library of Congress, Washington, DC
Reproduction number: LC-DIG-ppmsca-38818 (digital file from original item)
LC-USZ62-16767 (b&w film copy neg.)
Public Domain Source: http://hdl.loc.gov/loc.pnp/cph.3a53178

In March of 1925, Black intellectuals and artists took a major step forward in re-establishing a fair and equitable understanding of Black people. This effort took shape in an issue of the literary journal *Survey Graphic*, with the cover headline, "Harlem: Mecca of the New Negro"[56] (fig. 87). The magazine was edited by the Harvard-educated African American philosopher Alain LeRoy Locke (fig. 88), who sought the "spiritual emancipation" of Blacks through visual art. A primary arbiter of the Harlem Renaissance, Locke deemed the fine arts a potent vehicle for reconfiguring the image and identity of Blacks. Locke outlined his strategy in his essay, "The Art of the Ancestors," in which he urged Black artists to take pride in their African artistic heritage rather than look to European models for inspiration.[57] He pointed out that the

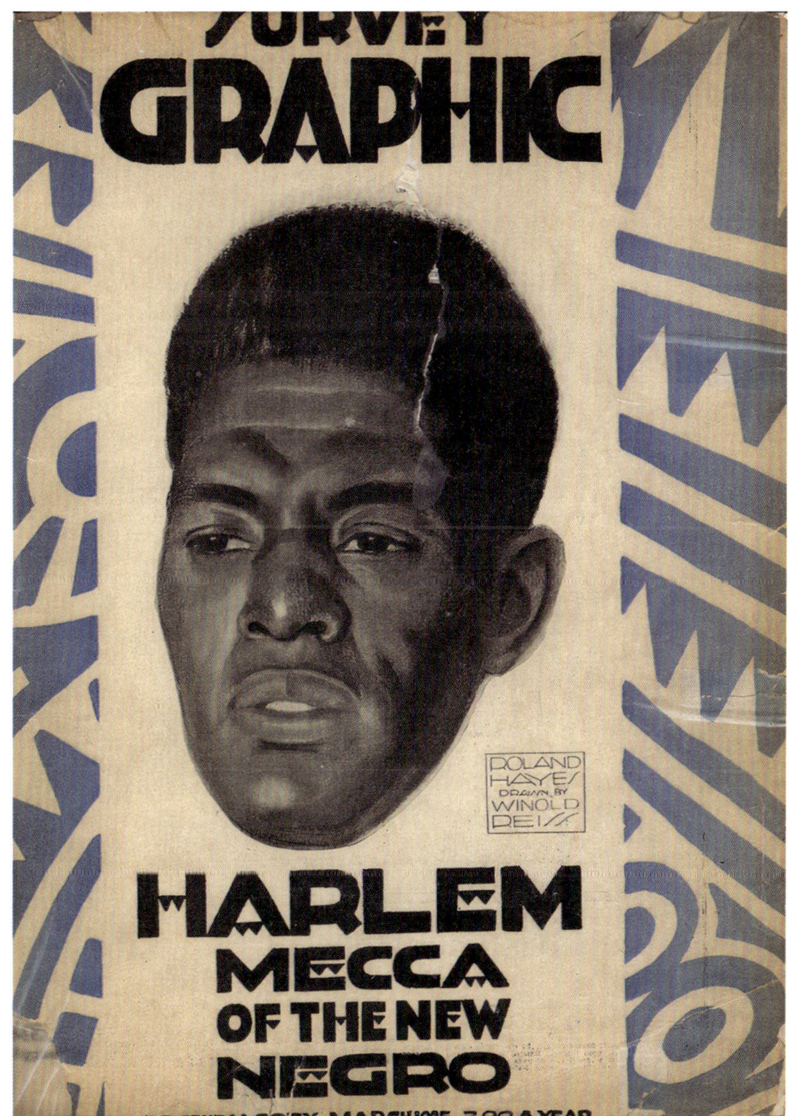

Fig. 87

RIGHT

Winold Reiss (German American, 1886–1953), "Harlem: Mecca of the New Negro," cover of *Survey Graphic* magazine 6, no. 6 (March 1925) with portrait of tenor Roland Hayes

Fig. 88

BELOW

Alain LeRoy Locke, ca. 1920
Collection of the Schomburg Center for Research in Black Culture, Photographs and Prints Division, The New York Public Library, New York, NY
Photograph courtesy of Wikimedia Commons Public Domain
Source: https://commons.wikimedia.org/wiki/File:Alain_LeRoy_Locke_(1885-1954).png)

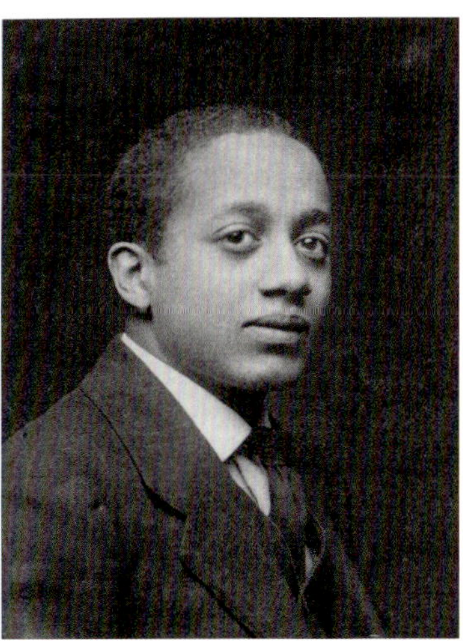

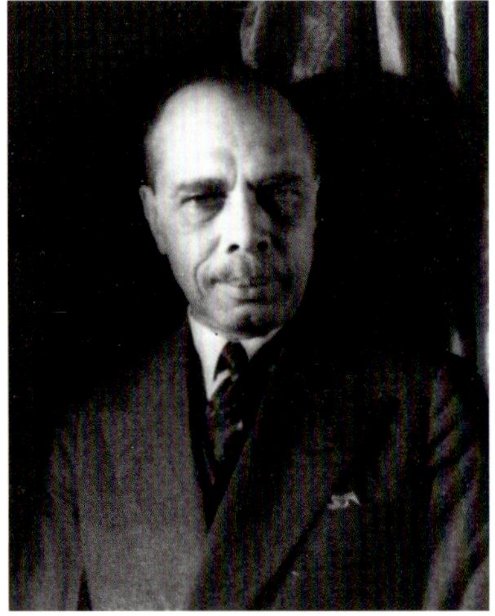

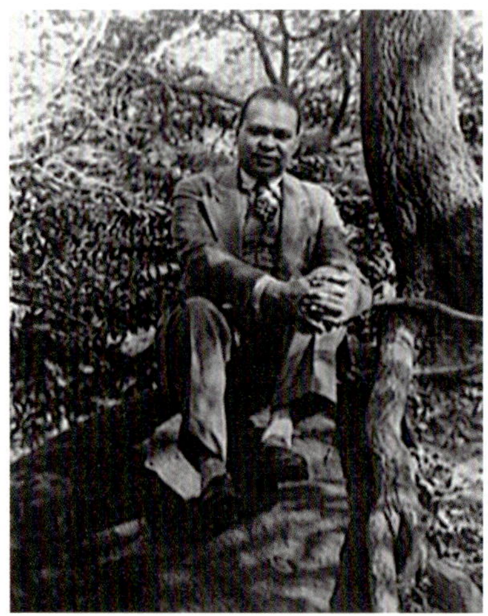

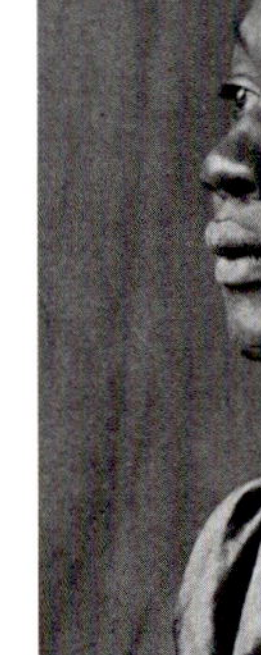

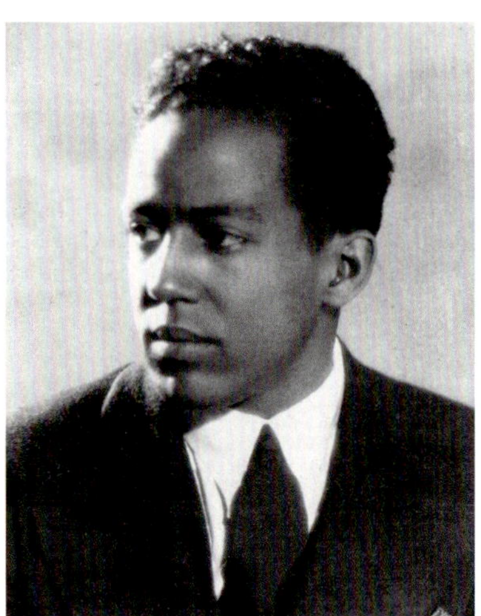

Fig. 89

TOP, LEFT

Carl Van Vechten (American, 1880–1964), *James Weldon Johnson*, 1932
Gelatin silver print
Collection of the Library of Congress, Washington, DC
LCCN2004663098.jpg
Public Domain Source: https://www.loc.gov/pictures/resource/cph.3a428F16/

Fig. 90

TOP, RIGHT

Carl Van Vechten (American, 1880–1964), *Countee Cullen*, in Central Park, June 20, 1941
Collection of the Library of Congress, Prints and Photographs Division
Washington, DC
Library of Congress Number: LC-USZ62-42529 (b&w film copy neg.)
Public Domain Source: https://www.loc.gov/pictures/item/2004662756/

Fig. 91

BOTTOM, LEFT

Portrait photograph of Claude McKay, 1920, unknown photographer
Public Domain Source Internet Archive identifier: springinnewhamp-00mckarich and Wikimedia at https://commons.wikimedia.org/wiki/File:Claude_McKay_1920.jpg)

Fig. 92

BOTTOM, RIGHT

Langston Hughes, ca. 1925,
Collection of the Schomburg Center for Research in Black Culture, Photographs and Prints Division, The New York Public Library, New York, NY
Public Domain Source: https://commons.wikimedia.org/wiki/File:Langston_Hughes_(1901-1967)_portrait.jpg

sculptures of traditional African artists had been "discovered" by avant-garde European artists at the turn of the twentieth century and served as inspiration for the art of, among several, renowned artists such as Spanish Cubist Pablo Picasso and French Fauvist Henri Matisse. Therefore, it seemed logical to Locke that African sculpture should also be inspirational to contemporary Black artists. In response to Locke's call to action, Black artists throughout the diaspora, particularly in the United States, embraced African sculptural models as a source of creative inspiration; and they looked to the "Black Experience" as subject matter.[58]

The Harlem issue of *Survey Graphic* featured thirty cultural and sociological essays and poems by Locke, Du Bois, NAACP (National Association for the Advancement of Colored People) co-founder James Weldon Johnson (fig. 89), and renowned Black poets and authors such as Countee Cullen (fig. 90), Claude McKay (fig. 91), Langston Hughes (fig. 92), and Jean Toomer.

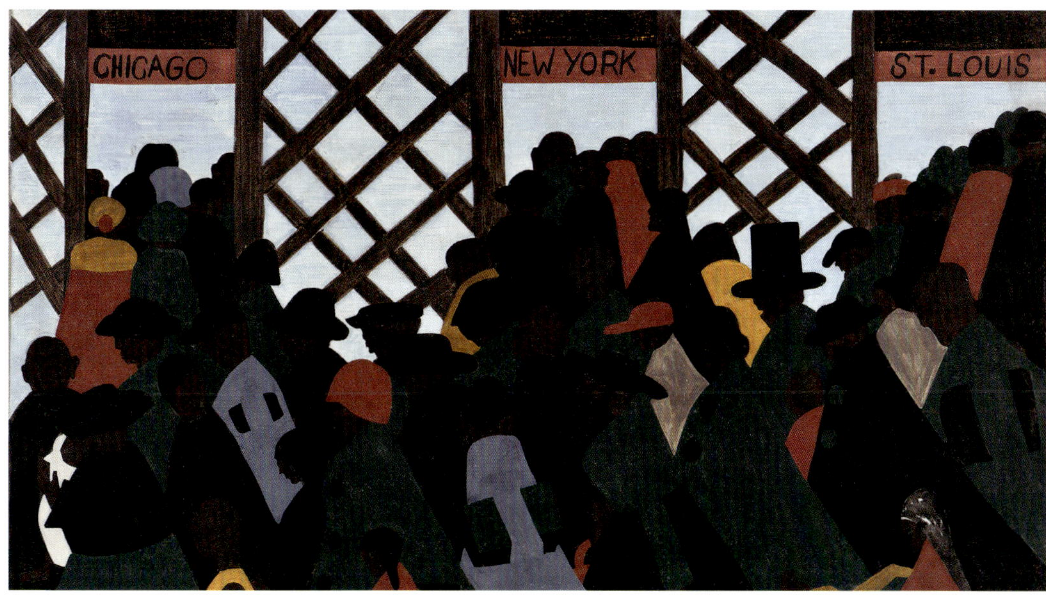

Fig. 93

Jacob Lawrence (American, 1917–2000), *Migration Series, Panel 1: During World War I There Was a Great Migration North by Southern African Americans*, 1940–1941, detail of Panel 1
Casein tempera on hardboard
12 x 18 in. (30.5 x 45.7 cm)
The Phillips Collection, Washington, DC
Acquired 1942; © 2022 The Jacob and Gwendolyn Knight Lawrence Foundation, Seattle / Artists Rights Society (ARS), New York, NY

Also included were photographs of African sculpture from the collection of wealthy White philanthropist Albert C. Barnes, as well as portrait sketches of "Harlem types" by the German artist Winold Reiss, who served as art director for the issue. Reiss's design for the magazine's cover featured a sensitive portrayal of renowned Black operatic tenor Roland Hayes as the "New Negro" and a combination of African and Art Deco design elements. In just two weeks, the journal sold an unprecedented 40,000 copies to mostly White subscribers and became the manifesto of the era. The persuasive power of the journal drew widespread attention to Black culture and launched a century-long campaign to change the image of Blacks from negative back to positive. One of the artists most influenced by Locke's views and the goals of the Harlem Renaissance was Jacob Lawrence. His documentation of the migration of one million Blacks from the Jim Crow South to what they hoped (wrongly) would be racism-free northern cities—the iconic *Migration Series* (fig. 93) now in the collection of the Museum of Modern Art in New York and the Phillips Collection in Washington, DC—is a definitive example of art designed to enlighten the world about the Black Experience.

The Latter Twentieth Century: The Pan-African Black Arts Movement

A subsequent concerted effort, through the medium of art, to correct the misperceptions of Blacks occurred with the Black Arts Movement. Influenced by a virtual maelstrom of civil unrest, particularly in the United States, many

Black artists felt compelled to create political art that addressed racial oppression. In 1961, at an annual meeting of the recently formed National Conference of Negro Artists, a leading Black artist, Elizabeth Catlett (fig. 94), made a widely influential speech, "The Negro People and American Art at Mid-Century." She issued a directive to Black artists to create art that would "express . . . racial identity, communicate with the Black community, and participate in struggles for social, political, and economic equality." Catlett's moving speech sparked a surge of politically engaged art and numerous Black arts groups were formed.[59]

Among these was Spiral, a cooperative of Black artists founded in 1963 by Romare Bearden (fig. 95), Charles Alston (fig. 96), Hale Woodruff (fig. 97), Ernest Crichlow, Felrath Hines, Richard Mayhew, James Yeargans, Alvin Hollingsworth, Reginald Gammon, and Merton Simpson. The name "Spiral" was chosen by Woodruff and referred to the spiral of Archimedes, a third-century BCE Greek mathematician who conceived of an abstract vortex that remained in perpetual motion. One of several catalysts for Spiral's founding was the 1963 March on Washington, during which Martin Luther King, Jr., delivered his legendary "I Have a Dream" speech, and a quarter-of-a-million demonstrators voiced their indignation at the persistence of racial oppression.[60] Reginald Gammon's iconic *Freedom Now* (fig. 98) was featured in the 1965

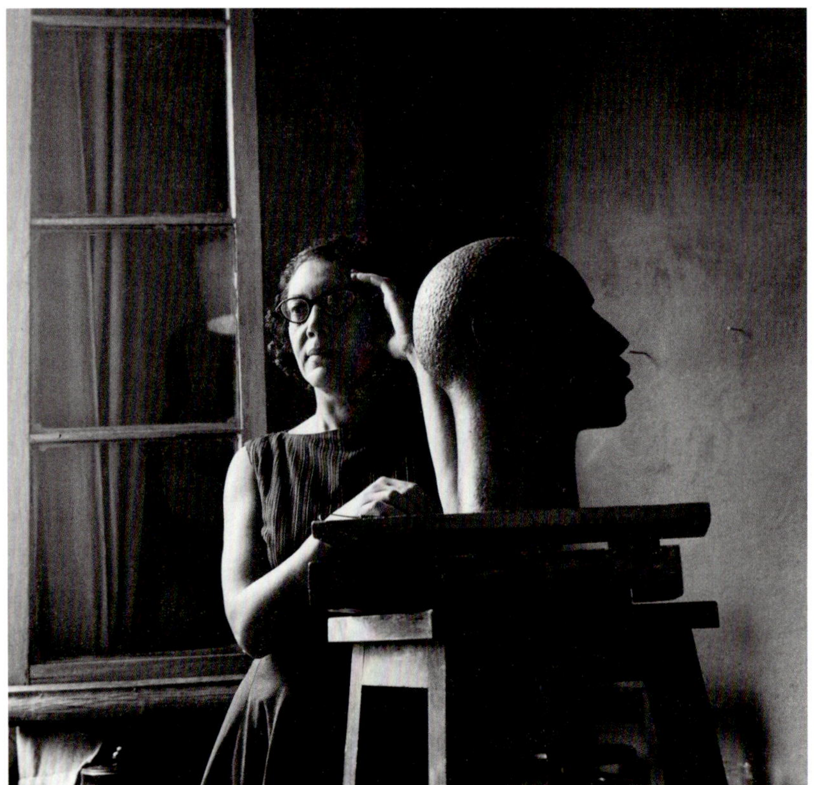

Fig. 94

Mariana Yampolsky (Mexican American, 1925–2002), *The Sculptor (Elizabeth Catlett)*, ca.1949, printed ca. 1990
Black-and-white photograph, gelatin silver print
Image: 8⅝ x 8¾ in. (21.9 x 22.3 cm); sheet: 1015/16 x 1315/16 in. (27.8 x 35.4 cm)
National Portrait Gallery, Smithsonian Institution, Washington, DC; S/NPG.91.74

Fig. 95

OPPOSITE, LEFT

Carl Van Vechten (American, 1880–1964), *Romare Bearden*, April 15, 1944
Photograph Photograph coutesy of Wikimedia Commons; Public Domain
Source: http://memory.loc.gov/cgi-bin/query/r?ammem/vv:@field(SUBJ+@band(Bearden,+Romare,--1911-1988+)

Fig. 96

OPPOSITE, MIDDLE

Andrew Herman, *Charles Alston*, January 1, 1939
Black and white photographic print
8¼ x 9⅞ in. (21 x 25 cm)
Created for the Federal Art Project, Photographic Division collection, ca. 1920–1965, bulk 1935–1942
Collection of the Archives of American Art, Public Domain
Source: https://commons.wikimedia.org/wiki/File:Archives_of_American_Art_-_Charles_Alston_-_2465_CROPPED.jpg)

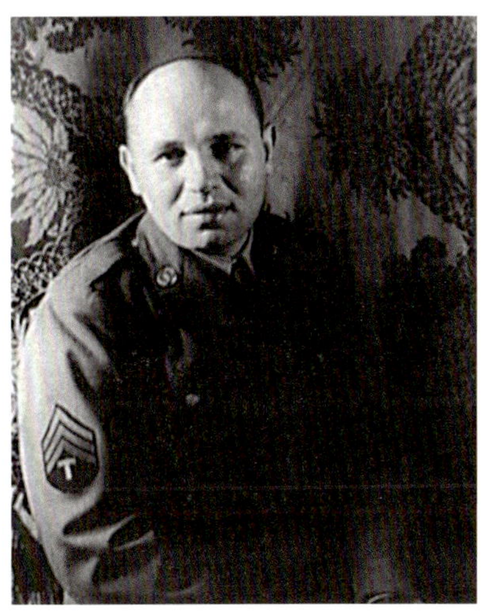

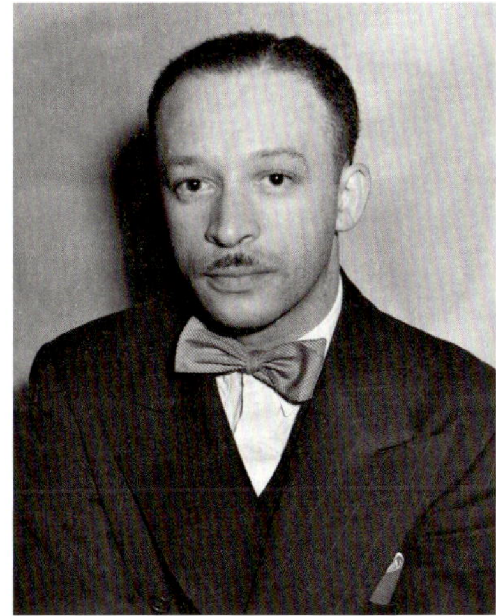

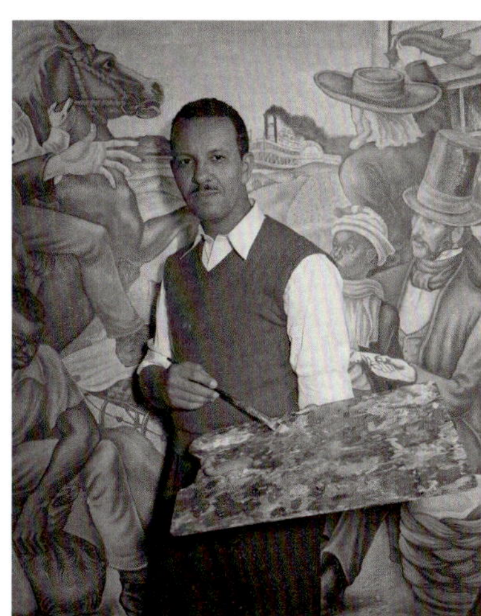

Fig. 97

FAR RIGHT

The painter Hale Woodruff
Collection of the Library of Congress
Prints and Photographs Division
Washington, DC
Digital ID: (digital file from intermediary roll film) fsa 8d02754 http://hdl.loc.gov/loc.pnp/fsa.8d02754;
Reproduction Number: LC-USW3-000265-D (b&w film neg)
Public Domain Source: https://www.loc.gov/pictures/resource/fsa.8d02754/)

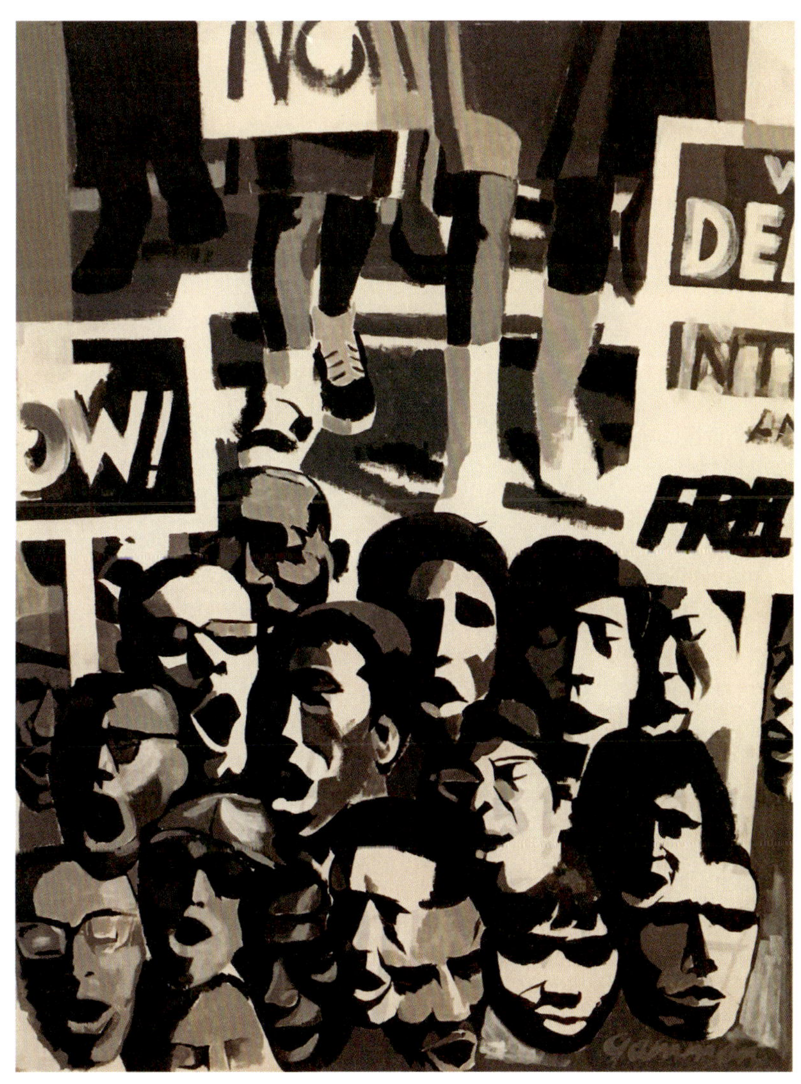

Fig. 98

Reginald Gammon (American, 1921–2005), *Freedom Now*, 1963
Acrylic on board
30 x 40 in. (76.2 x 101.6 cm)
National Afro-American Museum & Cultural Center, Wilberforce, OH
Estate of Reginald Gammon, licensed by Artists Rights Society (ARS), New York, NY

Spiral show in New York and presents a throng of protest marchers, shouting and holding agitprop placards.

By the mid-1960s, a Black Arts Movement had begun and was formalized in a number of ways, such as through the organization of FESTAC (Festival of Arts and Culture), held first in Dakar, Senegal, in 1966 and then in Lagos, Nigeria, in 1977. In addition, museums dedicated to Black art were established across the United States. Among these were the Studio Museum in Harlem, the International Afro-American Museum in Detroit, the Anacostia Museum of Culture and History in Washington, DC, the Museum of African American Art in Los Angeles, and the Afro-American Historical and Cultural Museum in Philadelphia. Black-owned galleries were founded as well, including Kenkeleba House, Just Above Midtown (JAM) Gallery, Cinque Galleries (the latter founded by former Spiral members), the Weusi-Nyumba Ya Sanaa (Swahili for "people's house of art"), and Acts of Art Gallery, all located in New York City.[61]

The Black Emergency Cultural Council (BECC), the Art Workers Coalition (AWC), and the United Black Artists' Committee (UBAC) were also formed to protest the absence of Black art in mainstream museums. The Harlem-based WEUSI Artist Collective was founded and dedicated to art as activism. Taking its name from the Swahili word for "black," a key goal was to include African icons and designs in members' art and to incorporate African and African American history, culture, and social concerns into their visual narratives. The group established their own gallery, Weusi-Nyumba Ya Sanaa and exhibited at FESTAC '77 in Lagos.[62]

Another pivotal arts collective of the Black Arts Movement was the Organization of Black American Culture (OBAC, pronounced "obasi," derived from the Yoruba word for king, *oba*). The group was co-founded in Chicago in 1967 by artist and historian Jeff Donaldson, who was then a university professor. Donaldson was joined in OBAC by Africana Studies historian Abdul Alkalimat (then, Gerald McWorter); and writer and African American literary historian Hoyt Fuller. Devoted to the arts—music, writing, dance, theater—the visual-arts arm of OBAC created murals such as the now historic *Wall of Respect*, painted on an abandoned building on the South Side of Chicago in 1967 (fig. 99). Designed to pay homage to Black leaders and to bring an element of visual beauty to the then-depressed South Side, the mural was a collaborative effort consisting of eight panels and some fifty portraits.

Among these portraits were depictions of major sports figures like Muhammad Ali and Kareem Abdul-Jabbar; jazz and blues artists Billie Holiday, Miles Davis, and Sarah Vaughan; soul music artists James Brown and Aretha Franklin; civil rights activists Adam Clayton Powell, Jr., Marcus Garvey, Stokely Carmichael, and Malcolm X; actors Sidney Poitier and Cicely Tyson; and literati Amiri Baraka, Gwendolyn Brooks, and James Baldwin. Participating OBAC artists included Sylvia Abernathy, who was responsible

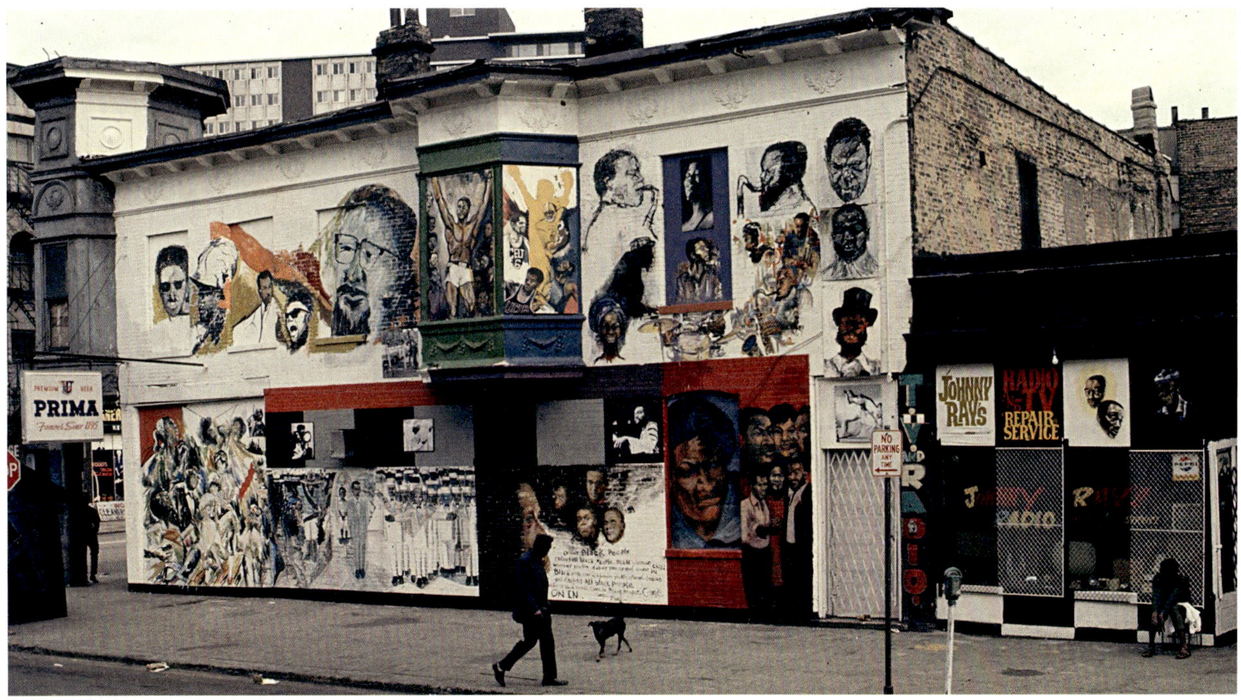

Fig. 99

Sylvia Abernathy, Barbara Jones-Hogu, Carolyn Lawrence, Myrna Weaver, Jeff Donaldson, Eliot Hunter, Wadsworth Jarrell, Norman Parish, William Walker, and others, *Wall of Respect*, 1967 (destroyed 1971)
Painted mural
Located at 43rd and Langley Streets, Chicago, IL Photograph © Robert A. Sengstacke

for the overall design of the mural, and Jeff Donaldson, who painted the "Jazz" panel. Wadsworth Jarrell contributed a panel on R&B artists; Barbara Jones-Hogu portrayed theater personalities; Norman Parish depicted Black statesmen; William Walker devoted his section to religious figures; and Carolyn Lawrence painted an homage to Black dancers on an adjacent newsstand. Sadly "The Wall" (as it was nicknamed) was destroyed when the building was demolished in 1971.[63]

In 1968, OBAC evolved first into the artists' group COBRA (Coalition of Black Revolutionary Artists) and, later, into AfriCOBRA (African Commune of Bad Relevant Artists). In the latter incarnation, this consortium identified common aesthetic goals. Their art emphasized narratives of Black history and the struggle for social, economic, and political parity. They utilized symbols, hieroglyphic writings, and textile designs derived from African sources and they strove for stylistic accessibility (words and recognizable figures) and a cohesive "look" that included a high-key palette of bright colors, bold patterns, visual improvisation, and jazz-inspired visual syncopation. Wildly popular during the late 1960s and 1970s, the AfriCOBRA visual approach became a hallmark of the Black Arts Movement and had far-reaching influence on artists throughout the United States and Europe for over a decade.[64]

AfriCOBRA artists organized a historic 1970 Conference on the Functional Aspects of Black Arts (CONFABA), in Evanston, Illinois.

Spearheaded by Donaldson at Northwestern University, the conference drew international attention to Black art. Approximately 50 scholars and artists from across the country participated in CONFABA. Participants formed a series of task forces to address five key areas: education, research, resources, dissemination, and aesthetics. Elizabeth Catlett addressed the CONFABA forum via telephone from her home in Mexico (she had been barred from returning to the United States for her unwillingness to comply with the demands of the HUAC—House Un-American Activities Committee—to identify suspected Communists). In her remarks, she described herself and her CONFABA compatriots as Black revolutionary artists who had to remain dedicated to the liberation of Black people from oppression. Catlett's address led to a major retrospective of her work at the Studio Museum in Harlem in 1971. After museum officials lobbied the State Department to grant Catlett a visa, she was at last

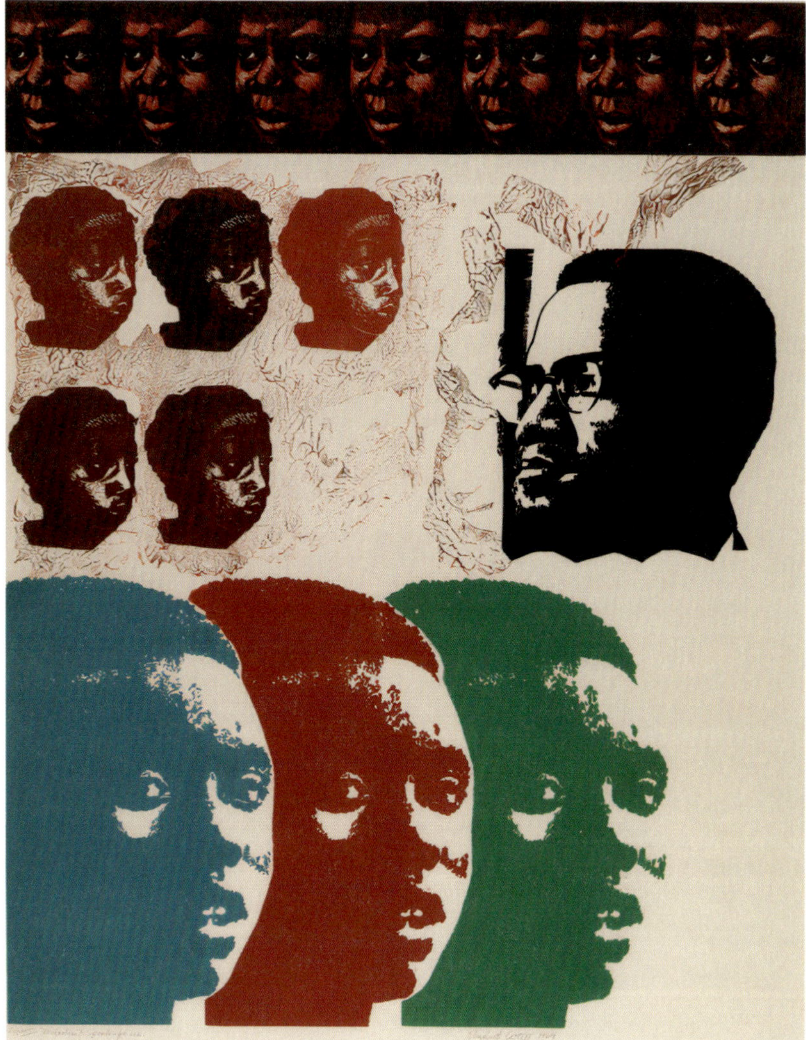

Fig. 100

Elizabeth Catlett (American, 1915–2012), *Malcolm X Speaks for Us*, 1969
Color linocut, serigraph, and monoprint
27 ½ x 27 ½ in. (69.8 x 69.8 cm)
The Pennsylvania Academy of Fine Arts, Philadelphia, PA
Gift of the Artist © Mora-Catlett Family / Licensed by Artists Rights Society (ARS), New York, NY

permitted to return to the United States for the opening of her show. The publicity surrounding the procurement of her visa and her retrospective catapulted Catlett into the national spotlight and earned her the title "foremother of the Black Arts Movement" and her art—images of minorities, political heroes (fig. 100), and the proletariat—was a testament to her politics.

The Twenty-first Century: Afrofuturism and Post-Black

The Black Arts Movement waned by the 1980s, but it had achieved its mission in concert with global political activism, most notably the end of apartheid in South Africa and changes taking place in the media, where Black journalists, filmmakers, actors, and writers became an ever-increasing presence after a century of protests against the exclusionary practices of those industries.[65] The repositioning of Blacks on a global stage appeared to culminate in the 2008 election of America's first Black president, Barack Obama. While occupying the White House with his family, Obama transformed perceptions of Blacks. In 2017, the National Portrait Gallery commissioned Amy Sherald to paint First Lady Michelle Obama's official portrait (fig. 101)—the first time ever that this prestigious task had been assigned to a Black artist.[66] Subsequently, in 2020, one of Sherald's paintings sold at auction for nearly $4.3 million, increasing the value of her work some thirty-fold—a testament to the power of visual art to create change and to record key moments in historical time.

A decade before Obama's election, a group of artists sought to re-envision the future of Blacks as unconnected to racial oppression and free of the history of enslavement—as if they could will that better future into existence. This group of creative thinkers and artists are known as Afrofuturists. A music, literary, film, and visual-arts movement, Afrofuturism comprises art that interrogates, deconstructs, and reimagines the past, present, and future of Africans in the diaspora through the lens of technoculture, science fiction, futuristic fantasy, and Eastern and African belief systems.[67] The term was first used in print in the mid-1990s by American literary critic Mark Dery in his book *Flame Wars: The Discourse of Cyberculture*, to describe artists and writers who envision a very different future for Blacks than that which anyone thus far has imagined. In response to Dery's question "Isn't the . . . future already owned by the technocrats and futurologists . . . —White to a man—who have engineered our collective fantasies?" Afrofuturist artists reply, "No." Their art defies the negatively constructed African past born of the slave trade and the seeming inevitability of its legacy in the future. They achieve this goal through the use of topsy-turvy takes on old themes, positive spins on once-negative icons, reimagined superheroes, and utopian future societies wherein time and space collapse and conflate and race becomes a malleable concept.[68]

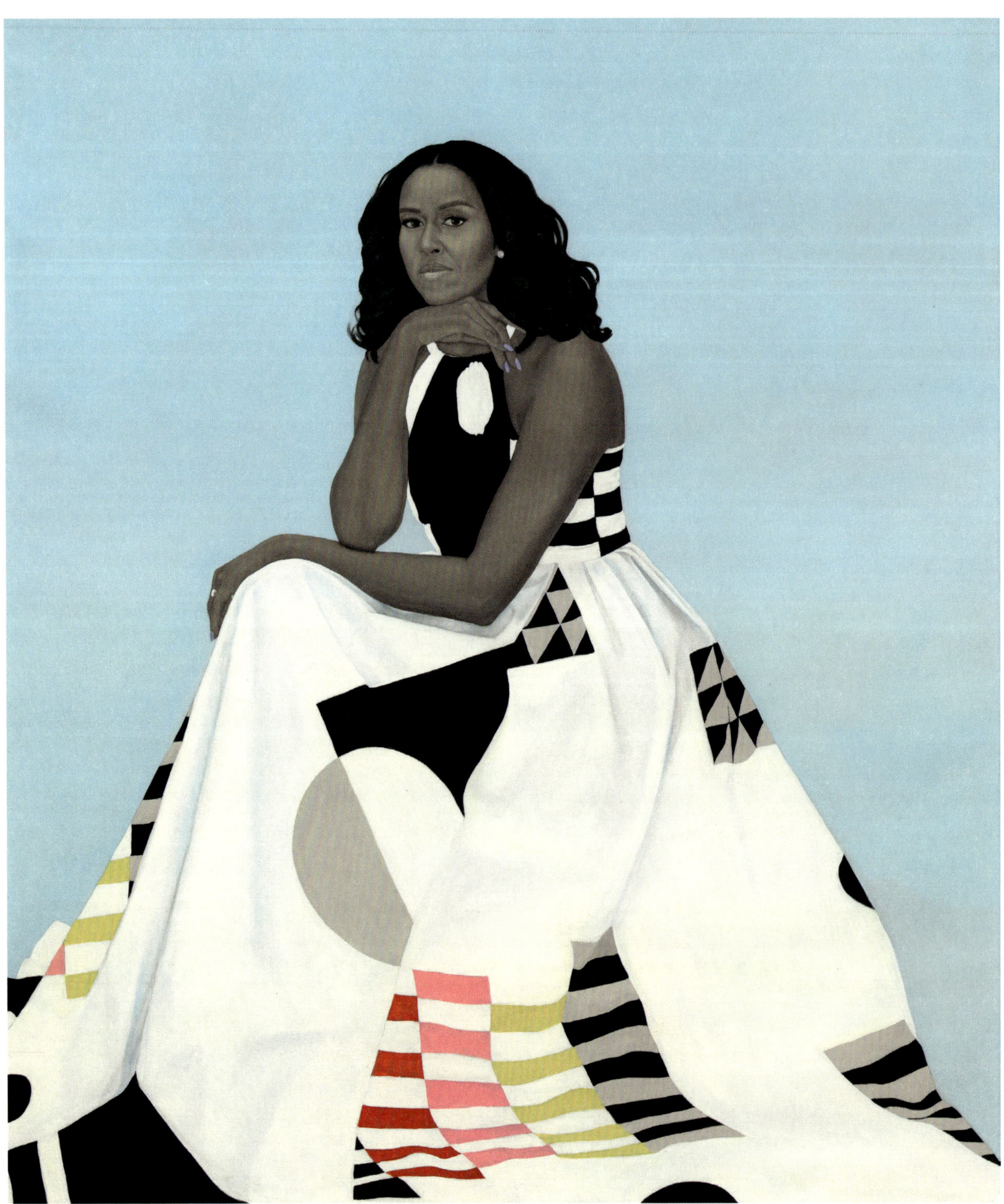

Fig. 101

Amy Sherald (American, 1973–),
Michelle LaVaughn Robinson Obama,
2018
Oil on linen
72⅛ x 60⅛ in. (183.2 x 152.7 cm)
National Portrait Gallery, Smithsonian Institution, Washington, DC
The National Portrait Gallery is grateful to the following lead donors for their support of the Obama portraits: Kate Capshaw and Steven Spielberg; Judith Kern and Kent Whealy; Tommie L. Pegues and Donald A. Capoccia
Image courtesy of the Smithsonian's National Portrait Gallery

Fig. 102

Still shot from the Netflix series *Bridgerton* created by Chris Van Duzen of Shonda Rhimes' production company, Shondaland
Center: actress Golda Rosheuvel as Queen Charlotte; right: Lady Danbury, played by Adjoa Andoh; left: Hugh Sachs as Brimsley

While many visual artists, musical artists, DJs, and writers are associated with Afrofuturism, arguably its most powerful manifestation has occurred in the movie industry with such blockbuster films as the Marvel-comics-based *Black Panther* starring the late Chadwick Boseman, and the wildly popular and award-winning streaming series *Bridgerton* (fig. 102). The former presents a fantasy world in which Blacks are the heroes, heroines, and technological and intellectual elite. The latter reimagines the past in which Blacks are an integral part of European high society and interracial marriage is the norm. Interestingly, Afrofuturism emerged coincident with the term "Post-Black" that was popularized in 2000 by Studio Museum Director Thelma Golden as a way of describing a world where cultural and social prejudices no longer affected the perception of Blacks.[69]

Related to Afrofuturism, Post-Black describes an ideal circumstance in which prejudice has not only been contested but eliminated and in which Black artists no longer feel compelled to use art as a form of social protest or ethnic self-expression. Not surprisingly, arguments have ensued over the validity of both the term "Post-Black" and the underlying belief that ethnic markers are no longer socio-economically or politically limiting. Proponents of a Post-Black era cite as evidence of the ebbing of Black identity politics the fact that a majority of White voters elected Barack Obama in 2008—and reelected him in 2012. For them, the sociopolitical changes that made Obama's presidency possible are proof positive that the age of identity politics in which Blacks have been so long immersed has seen its last days. Indeed, some social theorists saw

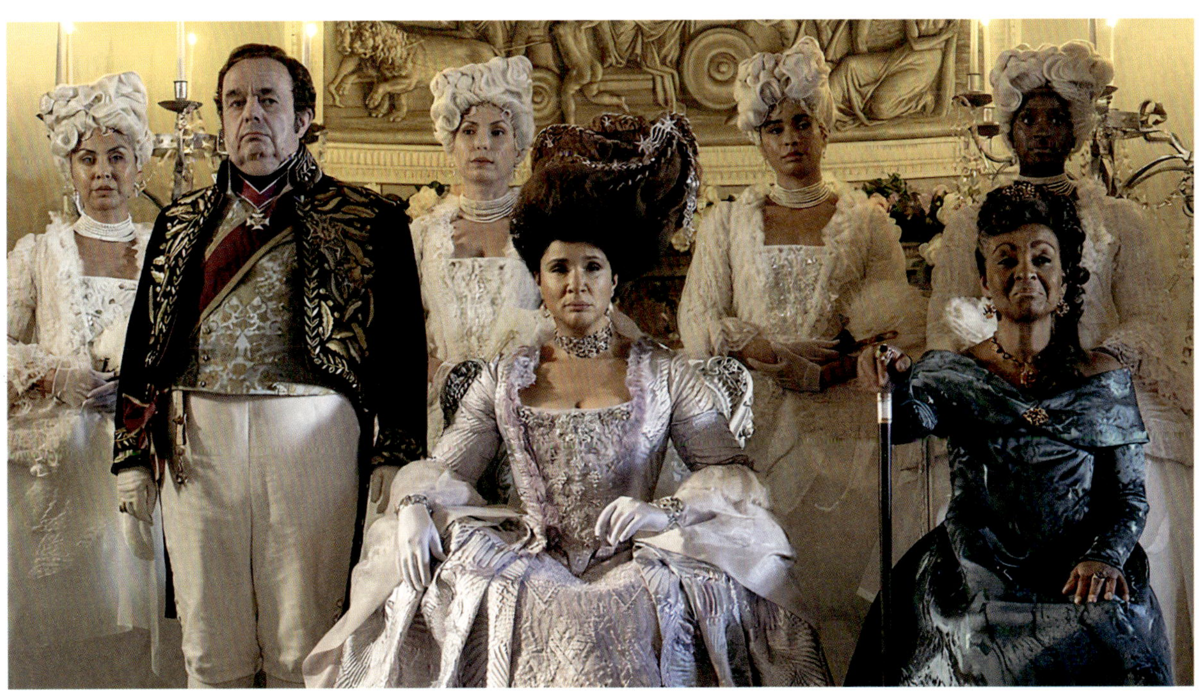

identity politics as a dated notion as early as the 1990s. This assessment was supported by the 2000 national census that revealed an increasing segment of the U.S. population had begun to reject racial labeling. "Other" had become the self-identification of choice for a growing number of Americans whose racial profiles were composites of two or more ethnicities, and many claimed entitlement to several cultural birthrights.[70]

Nevertheless, contradictory opinions persist as to whether or not a Post-Black era exists; and they tend to break along generational lines, with older Blacks who lived through the civil rights struggles of the twentieth century resisting what they perceive as the false hopes proffered by an alleged Post-Black age. The zeitgeist of younger Blacks, however—many of whom had yet to be born or, at best, were toddlers during the 1960s and 1970s—is vastly different from that of their predecessors. Social networking has transformed millions of formerly disconnected populations around the globe into Facebook and Twitter friends across cultural and ethnic boundaries. Twenty-first-century television as well as digital and print media are replete with mixed-race couples and biracial children, such as the pairing of the White, blond-haired Kelly Ripa with the Black ex-football player Michael Strahan as co-hosts of the Emmy Award winning television show *Live! With Kelly and Michael,* which, in 2014, was rated one of the most-watched syndicated talk shows in the country. In this new age, former President Obama's own biracial identity has prompted noticeable, positive shifts in American attitudes about miscegenation. Furthermore, readily accessible DNA analyses have exposed the fact that many African Americans share blood with their White compatriots.

That said, the best assessment as to whether or not an era of Post-Blackness is at hand can be found, not surprisingly, in visual culture—which, fortunately, speaks for itself. As an invaluable primary-source record, New Millennium visual culture tells us that racial identity is alive and well and that a bias-free, multicultural, Post-Black age has not yet been fully realized. Twenty-first-century artistic genres such as Afrofuturism reveal the persistence of identity politics. While Afrofuturists and their proponents consider race more fluidly and flexibly than did prior generations, they do not deny the existence of racial disparity. They do, however, allow for more nuanced and multiple ethnic influences to converge and for varying levels of racial tension and identity to coexist. Indeed, the fact that Black artists are still fantasizing about, and hoping for, a racist-free world is proof positive that such a world does not yet exist. Where we go from here is anyone's guess. Social progress is, and has always been, a forward and backward dance with no clear linear trajectory. Whatever happens, however, art will tell its Truth.

New York, NY
2024

NOTES

1. Donald Reid, "Anxieties about Race in Egyptology and Egyptomania, 1890–1960," Peabody Museum of Archaeology and Ethnology and Harvard Semitic Museum, 6 April 2017, Cambridge, MA, Harvard University, transcript and video, https://peabody.harvard.edu/video-anxieties-about-race-egyptology-and-egyptomania-1890%E2%80%931960 (accessed August 8, 2024).

2. Chiekh Anta Diop, *The African Origin of Civilization* (Brooklyn, NY: Lawrence Hill & Co., 1974).

3. Jean Devisse and Hugh Honour, *The Image of the Black in Western Art*, vols. 2, 4 (Cambridge, MA: Harvard University Press, 1979, 1989); Peter Mark, *Africans in European Eyes: Portrayal of Black Africans in Fourteenth and Fifteenth Century Europe* (Syracuse, NY: Syracuse University Press, 1974); Jan Neverdeen Pieterse, *White on Black: Images of Africa and Blacks in Western Popular Culture* (New Haven, CT: Yale University Press, 1995).

4. These terms were first used by Greeks in the fifth century, specifically Homer in the *Iliad* and the *Odyssey*, and in the writings of Herodotus. See Histories, 8.94, digital version in Perseus Digital Library online at https://www.perseus.tufts.edu/hopper/nebrowser?query=Perseus%3Atext%3A1999.01.0126&id=tgn%2C7000489 (accessed August 8, 2024). Note that this is, of course, an English translation—necessary for readers who do not read the original Greek and hence an example of a secondary source, however faithful to the original text.

5. Homer, *Odyssey*, 19: 246–248.

6. Diodorus Siculus, *Histories*, first century BCE, 3:9; Homer, *Iliad*, 1: 423–424.

7. Vitruvius, *On Architecture*, first century BCE, 1:10.

8. Ovid, "The Story of Perseus," *Metamorphoses*, books 4–5. Cepheus, Cassiopeia, and Andromeda are referred to as "Aethiopian" from the Greek words "aithein" (burned) and "ōps" (face). The name of the present-day African country of Ethiopia derives from this Greek reference to Black skin.

9. Ovid, "Andromeda rescu'd from the Sea Monster," *Metamorphoses*, book 4, 1 AD, translated by Sir Samuel Garth, John Dryden, et al., http://classics.mit.edu/Ovid/metam.4.fourth.html (accessed July 5, 2024).

10. Pieterse, *White on Black*, 23.

11. Genesis 2:13 identifies the name Cush (Kush) as a son of Ham, the son of Noah who populated Africa. See also 2 Chronicles 14:9; Isaiah 18:1–2; Job 28:19; Numbers 12:1.

12. According to chapter 2 of Greco-Roman (Greek-born) writer/philosopher Flavius Philostratus' (170–247 CE) book, *Lives of the Sophists* (2.558–559), Herodes erected a statue to each of his most beloved pupils.

13. John Aberth, *Plagues in World History* (Lanham, MD: Rowan & Littlefield, 2011); J.N. Hayes, *Epidemics and Pandemics: Their Impacts on Human History.* (New York: Bloomsbury Publishing, 2005).

14. Peter S. Well, *Barbarians to Angels: The Dark Ages Reconsidered* (New York: W. W. Norton, 2009); Conrad Leyser (Associate Professor of Medieval History, Oxford University, UK), "Barbarism and Superstition: The Middle Ages in Modern Times," Oxford University Faculty site, https://www.history.ox.ac.uk/barbarism-and-superstition-middle-ages-modern-times (accessed July 7, 2024).

15. Between 656–661 Caliph Ali forcibly took control of the Islamic Empire and was later assassinated.

16. Gábor Ágoston, *The Last Muslim Conquest: The Ottoman Empire and Its Wars in Europe* (Princeton: Princeton University Press, 2021).

17. Jack Goody, *Islam in Europe* (Cambridge, UK: Polity, 2013); Hichem Djaït, *Europe and Islam* (Berkeley: University of California Press, 1985), 89–97, 110–329.

18. Haroon Moghul, "The Late Great Mosque of Córdoba: When Islam and the West Were One." *Tikkun* 29.1 (2014): 34–40.

19. "Muslim Journeys | Item #218: 'Moors' from Oxford Islamic Studies Online," March 20, 2024. http://bridgingcultures-muslimjourneys.org/items/show/218 (accessed August 9, 2024).

20. Mark, *Africans in European Eyes*, 10–15; Pieterse, *White on Black*, 24–29.

21. Turold (?), *Song of Roland* (1040–1115). Only complete original copy held at the Bodleian Library at Oxford, England.

22. Pieterse, *White on Black*, 25.

23. Devisse, *The Image of the Black* , vol. 2, part 1, 81–148.

24. Coptic or African Christianity originated when Ethiopia was first evangelized by the apostles Saints Matthew and Bartholomew ca. 42 CE. See Otta Friedrich August Meinardus, "The Coptic Church: Its History, Traditions, Theology, and Structure," in *Two Thousand Years of Coptic Christianity* (Cairo, Egypt: American University in Cairo Press, 1999), p. 28.

25. Devisse, *The Image of the Black*, vol. 2, part 1, 81–148; Hans Werner Debrunner, *Presence and Prestige: Africans in Europe* (Basel: Basler Afrika Bibliographien, 1979), 24–25.

26. *Hallesches Heiltumsbuch*, manuscript, 1526–1527, Hofbibliothek, Aschaffenburg, Germany of the former relic collection of the church of Saints Maurice and Mary Magdalene in Halle, Saxony, Germany.

27. Pieterse, *White on Black*, 28.

28. Wolfram Von Eschenbach, *Parzival: A Knightly Epic*, translated by Jessie L. Weston (New York: G. E. Stechert & Co., 1912), reprint of the London 1894 edition.

29. Devisse, 64–75.

30. Pieterse, chapter 4.

31. Ibid.

32. "The Victorian era has found a central place in popular culture as a period of excessive sexual austerity, repression and prudery" marked by "Queen Victoria's insistence on propriety and respectability." Since the British could not openly act out sexual fantasies, they presumably "projected" (Freudian term) them onto their polar opposites—Black Africans—by making them carnal. See Stephen Garton, *Histories of Sexuality: Antiquity to Sexual Revolution* (Stocksfield, UK: Acumen, 2004), chapter 6, "Victorianism," 101–123; and Sigmund Freud, "On the Grounds for Detaching a Particular Syndrome from Neurasthenia Under the Description 'Anxiety Neurosis,' in J. Strachey, ed. and trans., *The Standard Edition of the Complete Psychological Works of Sigmund Freud* (London: Hogarth Press) 3rd ed., 85–115.

33. Dr. David Livingstone, *Livingstone's 1871 Field Diary*, updated edition in Livingstone Online, Adrian S. Wisnicki and Megan Ward, dirs., University of Maryland Libraries, 2017, at http://livingstoneonline.org/uuid/node/75c25c6c-c491-4059-b446-3562d7518c95 (accessed August 12, 2024).

34. Carolus (Carl) Linnaeus, *Systems Naturae* (1758; rpt. Göttingen: Vandenhoeck, 1772), quoted in Peter James Marshall and Glyndwr Williams, *The Great Map of Mankind: British Perceptions of the World in the Age of Enlightenment* (Cambridge, MA: Harvard University Press 1982), 245.

35. Ibid.

36. David Hume, "Of National Characters," in *The Philosophical Works of David Hume*, 4 vols. (Boston: Little, Brown and Co., 1854); Philip D. Curtin, *The Image of Africa: British Ideas and Action, 1780–1850*, vol. 1 (Madison, WI: University of Wisconsin Press, 1964), 1, 42.

37. Petrus Camper, *Dissertation physique de M. Pierre Camper* (Utrecht: Wild & Altheer, 1791); Johann Blumenbach, *On the Natural Variety of Mankind* (Göttingen: Heinrich Dietrich,1795; rpt. 1806); H.W. Debrunner, *Presence and Prestige: Africans in Europe* (Basel: Basler Afrika Bibliographien, 1979), 141–143, 301; Georg Wilhelm Friedrich, *Vorlesungen über die Philosophie der Geschichte* (Leipzig: P. Reclam, [1925?]; rpt. Stuttgart: Reclam, 1949, [1961]), 137–140; Pieterse, *White on Black*, 34, 40.

38. Phyllis J. Jackson, "(In)forming the Visual: (Re)presenting Women of African Descent," *International Review of African American Art* 14, no. 3 (1997): 34; Jean Devisse and Hugh Honour, *The Image of the Black in Western Art* (Cambridge, MA:

Harvard University, 1979, 1989) vol. IV, part 1, 52; Sander L. Gilman, *Difference and Pathology: Stereotypes of Race, Sexuality and Madness* (Ithaca: Cornell University Press, 1985).

39. Toby Appel, *The Cuvier-Geoffroy Debate: French Biology in the Decades Before Darwin* (New York: Oxford University Press, 1987); John P. Jackson and Nadine Weidman, *Race, Racism, and Science: Social Impact and Interaction* (NJ: Rutgers University Pres, 2005) 41–42; Jennifer Terry, *Deviant Bodies: Critical Perspectives on Difference in Science and Popular Culture* (Bloomington: Indiana University Press, 1995), 19–39.

40. Georges-Louis Leclerc, Comte de Buffon, *Histoire naturelle, générale et particulière*, vol. 3 (Paris: Royal Imprint, 1749).

41. Petrus Camper, *Dissertation physique de M. Pierre Camper* (Utrecht: Wild & Altheer, 1791); Johann Blumenbach, *On the Natural Variety of Mankind* (Göttingen: Heinrich Dietrich,1795; rpt. 1806); H.W. Debrunner, *Presence and Prestige: Africans in Europe* (Basel: Basler Afrika Bibliographien, 1979), 141–143, 301; Georg Wilhelm Friedrich, *Vorlesungen über die Philosophie der Geschichte* (Leipzig: P. Reclam, [1925?]; rpt. Stuttgart: Reclam, 1949, [1961]), 137–140; Pieterse, *White on Black*, 34, 40.

42. Charles Darwin, *On the Origin of Species by Means of Natural Selection, Or, The Preservation of Favoured Races in the Struggle for Life* (London: John Murray, 1859).

43. Darwin, *The Descent of Man and Selection in Relation to Sex* (London: John Murray, 1871).

44. Darwin traveled only once to Africa, on the HMS Beagle to the Cape of Good Hope where, from June 3 to 18, 1836, he visited with Sir George Hershel, a British diplomat in charge of the Royal Observatory.

45. Darwin, "Natural Selection," in *On the Origin of Species*, chapter 4, paragraph 6.

46. Ibid., paragraphs 12–14.

47. Ibid., paragraphs 21–34.

48. Herbert Spencer, *The Principles of Biology* (New York and London: D. Appleton and Company, 1864).

49. It remains a fact, even today, that darker skin is denigrated in many countries worldwide. Eastern women make wide use of bleaching creams, honor whiter-skinned movie actresses, and still cover their faces from the sun to avoid tanning. Racism was disseminated globally through cultural exchange supported by these known scholarly sources, rather than by Americans, Europeans, or anyone other than scholars reading the actual books. Consider how many people know about Darwin's theories but have never read his books.

50. David M. Goldenberg, *The Curse of Ham: Race and Slavery in Early Judaism, Christianity, and Islam Series: Jews, Christians, and Muslims from the Ancient to the Modern World* (NJ: Princeton University Press, 2003); Pieterse, "Children of Ham," in *White on Black*, 44.

51. Anonymous Franciscan friar, *Book of the Knowledge of All the Kingdoms Lands Lordships That Are in the World & the Arms & Devices of Each Land & Lordship or*

of the Kings and Lords Who Possess Them, ser. 2, vol. 29, trans. Clements Markham (London: Hakluyt Society, 1912); Mark, *Africans in European Eyes*, 36–37; Charles Darwin, *Origin of the Species* (New York: Burt, 1872).

52. Imanuel Geiss, *The Pan-African Movement: A History of Pan-Africanism in America, Europe and Africa, Africana Publishing Company* (New York: Holmes & Meier Publishers, 1974); Tony Martin, *Pan-African Connection: From Slavery to Garvey and Beyond* (Dover, MD: Majority Press, 1985); Marika Sherwood, *Origins of Pan-Africanism: Henry Sylvester Williams, Africa, and the African Diaspora* (London: Routledge, 2011).

53. Subsequent conferences were held in 1921 in Brussels, London, and Paris; in 1923 in Lisbon and London; in 1927 in New York City; and in 1945 in Manchester, UK.

54. Christopher Buck, "Harlem Renaissance" in *The American Mosaic: The African American Experience*. (Santa Barbara, CA: ABC-CLIO, 2013); Shannon King, *Whose Harlem Is This, Anyway? Community Politics and Grassroots Activism during the New Negro Era* (New York: New York University Press, 2015); Nathan Huggins, *Harlem Renaissance* (New York: Oxford University Press, 1973).

55. Christian Filostrat, *Negritude Agonistes* (Cherry Hill: NJ, Africana Homestead Legacy Publishers, 2008); Abiola Irele, "Négritude or Black Cultural Nationalism." *Journal of Modern African Studies* 3.3 (1965): 321–348; Bentley Le Baron, "Négritude: A Pan-African Ideal?" *Ethics* 76.4 (1966): 267–276; Lerebours, Michel-Philippe. "The Indigenist Revolt: Haitian Art, 1927–1944." *Callaloo*, 15, no. 3, (1992): 711–25; Eleanor Des Verney Sinette, *Arthur Alfonso Schomburg, Black Bibliofile & Collector: A Biography* (Detroit, MI: Wayne State University Press, 1989), 135.

56. "Harlem: Mecca of the New Negro," special issue of *Survey Graphic* 6, no. 6 (March 1925).

57. Alain Leroy Locke, "The Art of the Ancestors," in *Survey Graphic* 6, no. 6 (March 1925): 673.

58. Alain Leroy Locke, "Enter the New Negro," *Survey Graphic* 6, no. 6 (March 1925), 631; see also Locke, "The Legacy of the Ancestral Arts," in *The New Negro: An Interpretation* (1925; rpt. New York: Atheneum, 1968), 254–267.

59. Melanie Herzog, *Elizabeth Catlett: An American Artist in Mexico* (Seattle and London: University of Washington Press, 15–18, 20–21, 24–29, 47, 49, 50, 52, 53, 76; Elizabeth Catlett, interview with Gloria Van Scott, December 8, 1991, Cuernavaca, Mexico; Catlett, audiotaped interview with Melanie Herzog, June 14, 1991, Cuernavaca, Mexico, published in Herzog, *Elizabeth Catlett*, 15.

60. Romare Bearden and Harry Henderson, *A History of African American Artists from 1792 to the Present* (New York: Pantheon, 1993), 186, 200, 316, 400–402.

61. Lisa Farrington. *Creating Their Own Image: The History of African American Women Artists* (New York: Oxford University Press, 2006), 125–131.

62. Ibid., chapter 6; see also Farrington, *African American Art: A Visual and Cultural History* (New York: Oxford University Press), chapter 10.

63. Farrington, *African American Art*, chapter 10.

64. Ibid.

65. Eran Shor, Arnout van de Rijt, *Racial Bias in Media Coverage: Accounting for Structural Position and Public Interest, European Sociological Review*, 2023, jcad031, https://doi.org/10.1093/esr/jcad031 (accessed August 12, 2024); Richard G. Hatcher, "Mass Media and the Black Community," *The Black Scholar* 5, no. 1 (1973): 2–10, JSTOR, http://www.jstor.org/stable/41065597 (accessed August 12, 2024; Maryann Erigha, *The Hollywood Jim Crow: The Racial Politics of the Movie Industry* (New York University Press, 2019).

66. African American artist Kehinde Wiley was simultaneously awarded the commission for Barack Obama's presidential portrait.

67. Ytasha L. Womack, *Afrofuturism: The World of Black Sci-Fi and Fantasy Culture* (Chicago Review Press / Lawrence Hill Books, 2013); Aaron X. Smith, ed., *Afrocentricity in AfroFuturism: Toward Afrocentric Futurism* (Jackson: University of Mississippi Press, 2023).

68. Ibid.; Mark Dery, "Black to the Future: Interviews with Samuel R. Delany, Greg Tate and Tricia Rose," *Flame Wars: the Discourse of Cyberculture* (Duke University Press, 1995), 179–222; Farrington, *African American Art*, 375–382.

69. Farrington, *African American Art*, chapter 14.

70. Ibid.

Acknowledgments

The Farrington Family, for always being there.

Clark French, Principle Supporter of this project.

Agnes Gund, Principle Supporter of this project; Nicole Gallo, Curator, Agnes Gund Collection; and Sara Saltzman, Philanthropic Advisor to Agnes Gund.

The New York Community Trust: John Silberman, Partner, Silberman Zaretsky PC, Principal Supporter of this project.

Phong H. Bui, Publisher and Artistic Director of The Brooklyn Rail.
Jack Flam, past President and CEO, Dedalus Foundation, and Distinguished Professor Emeritus, City University of New York Graduate Center, for his endless support.

Leslie Pell Van Breen, Executive Director, The Artist Book Foundation (TABF), for her vision.

Lucia Garbatini, Advancement Office, The Artist Book Foundation, for connecting me with TABF.

Lisa Jones Gentry, Senior Counsel, Howard University, who first gave me the idea to create this book.

Jan Nederveen Pieterse, Suzanne and Duncan Mellichamp Chair and Distinguished Professor of Global Studies and Sociology at University of California Santa Barbara, for his brilliant and inspirational scholarship.

Erin Thompson, Attorney and Professor of Art History, City University of New York, John Jay College of Criminal Justice, for her contribution to this book.

David Bindman, Henry Louis Gates, Jr., Suzanne Preston Blier, Alejandro de la Fuente, and all the authors of the Harvard University Press series, *The Image of the Black in Western Art*, for their inspirational scholarship.

Go Fund Me contributors to this project, for their generous and unselfish support (including unnamed anonymous donors): Dorian Bergen, Richard Blondet, Alison Borrero, Sarajane Brittis, Claudia Calirman, Brian Cooper, Harold A. Dow, Gaye Ellington, Duane Farrington, Leslie Farrington, Frank Gimpaya, Tammi Lawson, Hilda Medina.

Teaching Guide and Sample Syllabus

The World Before Racism: An Art Story

Course Description:

The term *racism* is understood to mean that race is the principal determinant of specific human traits and capacities and that due to racial differences, one race is inherently superior to all others. Over time, racism has commonly referenced the notion that the White race is superior to all others, fostering prejudice and discrimination. *The World Before Racism: An Art Story* follows author and art historian Lisa Farrington's meticulous examination of the intersection of art, history, and race using original works of art as primary-source materials to support the thesis that racism is a construct, invented in the mid-1700s, to support the financial, political, and religious structures of European colonialism. Using art from ancient Egypt, classical Greece, and the Roman Empire, through medieval Europe and the colonization of the New World, to the art of the present day—sources that cannot be easily altered, edited, or selectively translated—the course expertly examines the intricate interplay between Black and White races and how they saw and understood each other over the centuries. The artworks serve as powerful voices, precisely conveying the artist's intended messages. The goal of *The World Before Racism: An Art Story* is to present irrefutable evidence that the ideology of racism is unfounded, unsupported, unjustified, and destined to fade away like so many other unprincipled ideas. Classes will include slide presentations, lectures, and class discussions.

Required Coursework:

1. Class participation
2. Art project
3. Quizzes on readings
4. Annotated bibliography
5. Oral presentation
6. Final project: Art exhibit design

Required Text:

Farrington, Lisa. *The World Before Racism: An Art Story*. North Adams, MA: The Artist Book Foundation, 2024.

Farrington, Lisa. *African American Art: A Visual and Cultural History*. Oxford, UK: Oxford University Press, 2017.

Additional Reading:

Bindman, David, and Henry Louis Gates, Jr., eds. *The Image of the Black in Western Art*. Cambridge, MA: Harvard University Press, 2010.

Gilman, Sander. *Difference and Pathology: Stereotypes of Sexuality, Race, and Madness*. Ithaca, NY: Cornell University Press, 1985.

Mark, Peter. *Africans in European Eyes: The Portrayal of Black Africans in Fourteenth and Fifteenth Century Europe*. Syracuse, NY: Syracuse University Press, 1974.

Pieterse, Jan N. *White on Black: Images of Africa and Blacks in Western Popular Culture*. New Haven: Yale University Press, 1992.

Lessons:

1. Art as a Primary Source

READING:

Jack Flam, "Introduction," in *The World Before Racism: An Art Story*

Lisa Farrington, "Art as a Primary Source," in *The World Before Racism: An Art Story*, Part 1

Lisa Farrington, "The Art of Perception: How Art Communicates," in *African American Art*, Chap. 1

2. A World Without Racism: Blacks in the Ancient World

READING:

Farrington, "The Ancient World," in *The World Before Racism: An Art Story*, Part 1

ADDITIONAL READING:

Frank Snowden, "Iconographical Evidence on the Black Populations in Greco-Roman Antiquity," in Bindman and Gates, *The Image of the Black in Western Art*, Vol. 1, Chap. 3

DISCUSSION QUESTION:

What was the status of Africans in Ancient Greece and Rome?

3. Race and Religion: Moors and Christianity

READING:

Farrington, "The Middle Ages and the Moors," in *The World Before Racism: An Art Story*, Part 2

ADDITIONAL READING:

Jean Devisse, "The Black and His Color: From Symbols to Realities," in Bindman and Gates, *The Image of the Black in Western Art*, Vol. 2, Part 1, Chap. 2

DISCUSSION QUESTION:

What effect did the rise of Christianity have on the image of Blacks and the idea of Blackness in Western thinking?

4. Old Masters and the Black Subject

READING:

Farrington, "From Gothic to Renaissance: St. Maurice and Parzival," in *The World Before Racism: An Art Story*, Part 2

ADDITIONAL READING:

Mark, *Africans in European Eyes*

DISCUSSION QUESTION:

Why did Africans become especially honored and appreciated in Europe from the late Middle Ages to the Renaissance?

5. Eighteenth Century: The Dark Continent and the Rise of White Supremacy

READING:

Farrington, "European Ascendency: From Slavs to Slaves," in *The World Before Racism: An Art Story*, Part 3

ADDITIONAL READING:

Pieterse, "In the Dark Continent," and "Colonialism and Western Popular Culture," in *White on Black*, Chaps. 4–5

DISCUSSION QUESTION:

What prompted the rise in racism and what purpose did it serve?

6. Nineteenth Century: Slavery and Abolition

READING:

Farrington, "Architects of Racism: Eighteenth and Nineteenth Centuries" in *The World Before Racism: An Art Story*, Part 3

ADDITIONAL READING:

Hugh Honour, "The Atlantic Triangle," in Bindman and Gates, *The Image of the Black in Western Art*, Vol. 4, Part 1, Chap. 1

DISCUSSION QUESTION:

What were the scientific bases for theories on racial hierarchy? What was Darwin's opinion on natural selection?

7. Nineteenth Century: The "Orient" and the "Other"

READING:

Pieterse, read the chapters "Servants: Sometimes a Moor" and "Libido in Color" in *White on Black*

ADDITIONAL READING:

Sander L. Gilman, "The Hottentot and the Prostitute: Toward an Iconography of Female Sexuality," in *Difference and Pathology: Stereotypes of Sexuality, Race, and Madness*, 76–109

DISCUSSION QUESTION:

List the stereotypes often associated with Blacks. Do these stereotypes apply to the Blacks you know personally?

8. The Harlem Renaissance: The "New Negro" Re-envisions Blackness

READING:

Farrington, "The Early Twentieth Century: The Harlem Renaissance," in *The World Before Racism: An Art Story*, Part 4

Farrington, "Modernism and the Harlem Renaissance," in *African American Art*, Chap. 6

DISCUSSION QUESTION:

What were the goals of the Harlem Renaissance and why?

ASSIGNMENT:

a) Choose a research topic on the Black image from the list at the end of the syllabus.

b) Select two or more scholarly books (or book chapters) on your topic.

c) List each book as a bibliographic entry.

d) Summarize ("annotate") each book (or chapter) in your own words.

9. The Black Arts Movement

READING:

Farrington, "The Latter Twentieth Century: The Pan-African Black Arts Movement," in *The World Before Racism. An Art Story*, Part 4

Farrington, "Pop and Agitprop: The Black Arts Movement," in *African American Art*, Chap. 10

DISCUSSION QUESTION:

What do you think prompted the Black Arts Movement and what were its goals?

10. Contemporary Trends: The Last Laugh

READING:

Farrington, "The Twenty-first Century: The Age of Afro-Futurism and Post-Black," in *The World Before Racism: An Art Story*, Part 4

Farrington, "Post-Black and the New Millennium," in *African American Art*

ASSIGNMENT:

Inspired by the readings, create a work of art that "deconstructs" or reimagines a racial stereotype, changing its original meaning.

DISCUSSION QUESTION:

How do you see the condition of White–Black race relations in the twenty-first century?

11–14. Student Oral Presentations

Present to the class a 15-minute oral report based on your researched topic.

The report should include a slide presentation of the images you discuss.

Presentations will be graded on audience engagement; quality and thoroughness; organization and clarity; familiarity with your subject (you may refer to notes, but reading from a prepared text is not acceptable); timing (no less than 15 minutes); and quality of the slide show.

15. Final Project: Exhibition Design Presentation

Note to Educators: Prior to this assignment, show your students examples of gallery installations, virtual or actual, to spark their creativity.

a) Choose a theme / title for an exhibition based on the class material.

b) Choose four artists for your exhibit who depict Black people in their work.

c) Describe 1) your theme; 2) why it's important; 3) what you hope to communicate to your audience.

d) Prepare a checklist of at least 10 artworks by the 4 artists to be included in your exhibition. The checklist should include a description of each work, including 1) title, 2) medium, 3) size, 4) year of creation, and 5) a description of each work's appearance or an actual picture of it.

e) In your own words, write a short biography of each artist.

f) Write or draw/design a description of the installation of the exhibition including:

i. the size and nature of your gallery space (room[s] size and configuration, wall color, lighting, etc.).

ii. where and how each work will be displayed (on the wall, on pedestals, which works will appear alone or grouped together, etc.).

iii. a description of any other important feature of your show you plan to include (video installation, wall labels, entrance plaque, etc.).

g) Write a review of your exhibition as if you were an art critic who had seen the show and was writing an essay for *The New York Times* or an art magazine.

h) Give a 5-minute presentation of your design to the class before submission for grading.

Research/Presentation Topics

1. Black Male Sexuality in Film
2. Black Male Aggression in Film
3. The Black Male Nude in Art
4. The Black Athlete: Myth and Reality
5. Jezebel: Black Female Sexuality in Film
6. Sapphire: Stereotypes of the Angry Black Woman
7. The Black Female Nude in Art
8. Black Women Fashion Models
9. Black Christian Saints and Kings
10. Ethiopians in Greek Literature
11. Blacks in American Literature
12. Black-Power Art of the 1960s
13. The Phenomenon of the Black Collectible
14. The Response to Black Culture in Asia
15. Blacks in Music Videos and Hip Hop Culture
16. Blacks in Contemporary TV Sitcoms
17. The Aunt Jemima Stereotype
18. The Black Comic and the Sambo Image
19. Black Stereotypes in Advertising
20. The News Media's Portrayal of Blacks
21. Myths of Lazy Native/Slave
22. The Black Family in Film
23. The Black Family and the Moynihan Report
24. Miscegenation: Interracial Scenarios in Film
25. The Tragic Mulatto in Film
26. Racism in Children's Books
27. Adrian Piper
28. Betye Saar and Aunt Jemima
29. Michael Ray Charles
30. Robert Colescott
31. Kara Walker
32. Faith Ringgold
33. Renee Cox
34. Black Homosexuality in the Photographs of Robert Mapplethorpe
35. Black Homosexuality in the Photographs of Lyle Ashton Harris
36. Black Women in Western Photography
37. Harlem Renaissance Fine Arts Images of Blacks
38. James van der Zee
39. Reginald Marsh
40. Jacob Lawrence
41. Romare Bearden
42. A professor-approved artist of your choice
43. A professor-approved topic of your choice

Bibliography

(See also the extensive bibliography at the end of Jan N. Pieterse's *White on Black: Images of Africa and Blacks in Western Popular Culture.*)

Arnold, Dorothea, Lyn Green, and James Allen. *The Royal Women of Amarna: Images of Beauty from Ancient Egypt.* New York: The Metropolitan Museum of Art, 1999.

Bearden, Romare, and Harry Henderson. *A History of African American Artists: From 1792 to the Present.* New York: Pantheon Books, 1993.

Betye Saar: Workers and Warriors, The Return of Aunt Jemima. New York: Michael Rosenfeld Gallery, 1998.

Bindman, David, and Henry Louis Gates, Jr. *The Image of the Black in Western Art.* Cambridge, MA: Harvard University Press, 2010.

Boime, Albert. *The Art of Exclusion: Representing Blacks in the Nineteenth Century.* Washington, DC: Smithsonian Institution Press, 1990.

Buck, Christopher. "Harlem Renaissance" in *The American Mosaic.* Santa Barbara, CA: ABC-CLIO, 2013.

Campbell, Dr. Mary Schmidt, Lucy R. Lippard, Eleanor Munroe, et al. *Faith Ringgold: 20 Years of Painting, Sculpture and Performance.* New York: Studio Museum of Harlem, 1984.

Dancing at the Louvre: Faith Ringgold's French Collection and Other Story Quilts. Exhibition catalogue. New York: New Museum, 1998.

Davis, Angela. *Women, Race & Class.* New York: Vintage Books, 1983.

Debrunner, H.W. *Presence and Prestige: Africans in Europe. A History of Africans in Europe before 1918.* Basel: Basler Afrika Bibliographien, 1979.

Dery, Mark. "Black to the Future" in *Flame Wars: the Discourse of Cyberculture.* Durham, NC: Duke University Press, 1994.

Diodorus Siculus. *Library of History.* First century BC, 3:9.

Diop, Cheikh A. *The African Origin of Civilization.* Brooklyn, NY: Lawrence Hill Books, 1974.

Djaït, Hichem. *Europe and Islam.* Berkeley, CA: University of California Press, 1985.

Driskell, David. *Harlem Renaissance: Art of Black America.* New York: Studio Museum in Harlem, 1987.

———. *Two Centuries of Black American Art.* Los Angeles: Los Angeles County Museum of Art, 1976.

Dubin, Steven C. "Symbolic Slavery: Black Representations in Popular Culture." *Social Problems* 34, no. 2 (April 1987).

Erigha, Maryann, *The Hollywood Jim Crow: Racial Politics of the Movie Industry.* New York: NYU Press, 2019.

Eschenbach, Wolfram V. *Parzival: A Knightly Epic.* Trans. by Jessie L. Weston. New York: G. E. Stechert & Co., 1912.

Farrington, Lisa E. *African-American Art: A Visual and Cultural History.* Oxford, UK: Oxford University, 2016.

———. *Creating Their Own Image: A History of African American Women Artists.* Oxford, UK: Oxford University Press, 2005.

Fine, Elsa Honig. *The Afro-American Artist: A Search for Identity.* New York: Holt, Rinehart & Winston, 1973.

Flomenhaft, E. *Faith Ringgold: A 25 Year Survey.* Roslyn, NY: Fine Arts Museum of Long Island, 1990.

Gaspar, David B., and Darlene Clark Hine. *More Than Chattel: Black Women and Slavery in the Americas.* Bloomington, IN: Indiana University Press, 1996.

Geiss, Imanuel. *The Pan-African Movement: A History of Pan-Africanism in America, Europe, and Africa.* New York: Holmes & Meier Publishers, Inc., 1974.

Gilman, Sander L. *Difference and Pathology: Stereotypes of Sexuality, Race, and Madness.* Ithaca, NY: Cornell University Press, 1985.

Giddings, Paula. *When and Where I Enter: The Impact of Black Women on Race and Sex in America.* New York: William Morrow and Company, 1984.

Goings, Kenneth W. *Mammy and Uncle Mose: Black Collectibles and American Stereotyping.* Bloomington, IN: Indiana University Press, 1994.

Golden, Thelma. *Black Male: Representations of Masculinity in American Art.* New York: Abrams Books, 1995.

Goldenberg, David M. *The Curse of Ham: Race and Slavery in Early Judaism, Christianity, and Islam.* Princeton, NJ: Princeton University Press, 2003.

Goody, Jack. *Islam in Europe.* Cambridge, UK: Polity, 2013.

Hatcher Richard G. "Mass Media and the Black Community." *The Black Scholar* 5, no. 1 (1973): 2–10.

Hernton, Calvin C. *Sex and Racism in America.* New York: Anchor Books, 1988.

Herzog, Melanie Anne. *Elizabeth Catlett: An American Artist in Mexico.* Seattle: University of Washington Press, 2000.

Homer, *Iliad*, 1: 423–3.

hooks, bell. *Black Looks: Race and Representation.* Boston: South End Press, 1992.

Huggins, Nathan. *Harlem Renaissance.* New York: Oxford University Press, 1973.

Irele, Abiola. "Négritude or Black Cultural Nationalism." *Journal of Modern African Studies* 3, no. 3 (1965): 321–348.

Jackson, Phyllis J. "(In)forming the Visual." *International Review of African American Art* 14, no. 3 (1997).

Jackson, John P., and Nadine Weidman. *Race, Racism, and Science.* New Brunswick, NJ: Rutgers University Press, 2005.

Jones, Jacqueline. *Labor of Love, Labor of Sorrow: Black Women, Work and the Family from Slavery to the Present.* New York: Basic Books, 1985.

Kaplan, Sydney. *The Portrayal of the Negro in American Painting.* Exhibition catalogue. Brunswick, ME: Bowdoin College, 1964.

Karageorghis, Vassos. *Blacks in Ancient Cypriot Art.* Houston, TX: Menil Foundation, 1988.

King, Shannon. *Whose Harlem Is This, Anyway? Community Politics and Grassroots Activism.* New York: NYU Press, 2015.

Le Baron, Bentley. "Négritude: A Pan-African Ideal?" *Ethics* 76, no. 4 (1966): 267–276.

Lerebours, Michel-Philippe. "The Indigenist Revolt: Haitian Art, 1927–1944." *Callaloo*, 15, no. 3, (Summer 1992): 711–725.

Lewis, Samella S. *African-American Art and Artists.* Berkeley, CA: University of California Press, 1990.

Locke, Alain LeRoy, ed. "Harlem: Mecca of the New Negro." Special issue of *Survey Graphic* 6, no. 6 (March 1925).

Locke, Alain LeRoy. *The Negro in Art: A Pictorial Record of the Negro Artist and of the Negro Theme in Art.* Hacker Art Books, 1940.

———. *The New Negro: An Interpretation.* New York: Boni Books, 1925.

Lorde, Audre. *Sister Outsider: Essays and Speeches.* Berkeley, CA: Crossing Press, 1984.

Mark, Peter. *Africans in European Eyes: The Portrayal of Black Africans in Fourteenth and Fifteenth Century Europe.* Syracuse, NY: Maxwell School of Citizenship and Public Affairs, Syracuse University, 1974.

Martin, Tony. *Pan-African Connection: From Slavery to Garvey and Beyond.* Dover, MA: The Majority Press, 1985.

McElroy, Guy C. *Facing History: The Black Image in American Art.* Washington, DC: The Corcoran Gallery, 1990.

Morton, Patricia. *Disfigured Images: The Historical Assault on Afro-American Women.* Westport, CT. Praeger Publishers, 1996.

Parry, Ellwood. *The Image of the Indian and the Black Man in American Art.* George Braziller, Inc., 1974.

Pieterse, Jan N. *White on Black: Images of Africa and Blacks in Western Popular Culture.* New Haven: Yale University Press, 1992.

Patton, Sharon. *African American Art.* Oxford, UK: Oxford University Press, 1998.

Powell, Richard J. *Black Art and Culture in the 20th Century.* London, UK: Thames and Hudson, 1997.

Pinder, Kymberly N., ed. *Race-ing Art History: Critical Readings in Race and Art History.* Oxfordshire, UK: Routledge, 2002.

Sherwood, Marika. *Origins of Pan-Africanism.* Oxfordshire, UK: Routledge, 2011.

Shor, Eran, and Arnout van de Rijt. "Racial Bias in Media: Accounting for Structural Position and Public Interest." *European Sociological Review* 40, no. 4 (August 2024): 652–671. https://doi.org/10.1093/esr/jcad031 (accessed August 14, 2024).

Smith, Aaron X., ed., *Afrocentricity in AfroFuturism: Toward Afrocentric Futurism.* Jackson, MS: University Press of Mississippi, 2023.

Terry, Jennifer, and Jacqueline L. Urla, eds. *Deviant Bodies: Critical Perspectives on Difference.* Bloomington, IN: Indiana University Press, 1995.

Vitruvius, *On Architecture.* First century BCE. 1: 10.

Wallace, Michele. *Black Macho and the Myth of the Superwoman.* London and New York: Verso, 1991.

———. *Black Popular Culture.* Seattle: Bay Press, 1992.

———. *Invisibility Blues: From Pop to Theory.* London and New York: Verso, 1990.

Wells, Peter S. *Barbarians to Angels: The Dark Ages Reconsidered.* New York: W. W. Norton & Company, 2009.

Willis, Deborah. *Picturing Us: African American Identity in Photography.* New York: New Press, 1994.

Willis, Deborah, and Carla Williams. *The Black Female Body: A Photographic History.* Philadelphia: Temple University Press, 2002.

Womack, Natasha L. *Afrofuturism: The World of Black Sci-Fi and Fantasy Culture.* Chicago: Lawrence Hill Books, 2013.

Index

Page numbers in *italics* refer to illustrations.

C

D

E

F

G

H

V

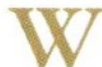

Z

First Edition

Published in the United States by
The Artist Book Foundation
1327 MASS MoCA Way, North Adams, MA 01247

Distributed in the United States, its territories and possessions, and Canada by National Book Network, Inc.

Distributed outside North America by National Book Network, Inc.

Publisher and Executive Director: L. Pell van Breen
Art and Production Director: David Skolkin
Design: Sophie Gerry
Editor: Deborah Thompson
Proofreader: Nicole Barone
Indexer: Barbara Smith
Printed in Italy

Library of Congress Cataloging-in-Publication Data

Names: Farrington, Lisa E., author. | Flam, Jack D., writer of introduction. | Thompson, Erin L., writer of foreword.
Title: The world before racism : an art story / by Lisa Farrington ; essays by Jack Flam and Erin Thompson.
Description: First. | North Adams : The Artist Book Foundation, 2025. |
Identifiers: LCCN 2024036308 (print) | LCCN 2024036309 (ebook) | ISBN 9798987228272 (hardback) | ISBN 9798987228265 (ebook)
Subjects: LCSH: Art and race. | Race relations--History. | Black people in art. | White people in art.
Classification: LCC N5303 .F28 2025 (print) | LCC N5303 (ebook) | DDC 701/.03--dc23/eng/20240820
LC record available at https://lccn.loc.gov/2024036308
LC ebook record available at https://lccn.loc.gov/2024036309

ISBN: 979-8-9872282-7-2
eISBN: 979-8-9872282-6-5

Cover image: Detail of fig. 74
p. 2: Fig. 41
p. 4: Fig. 75